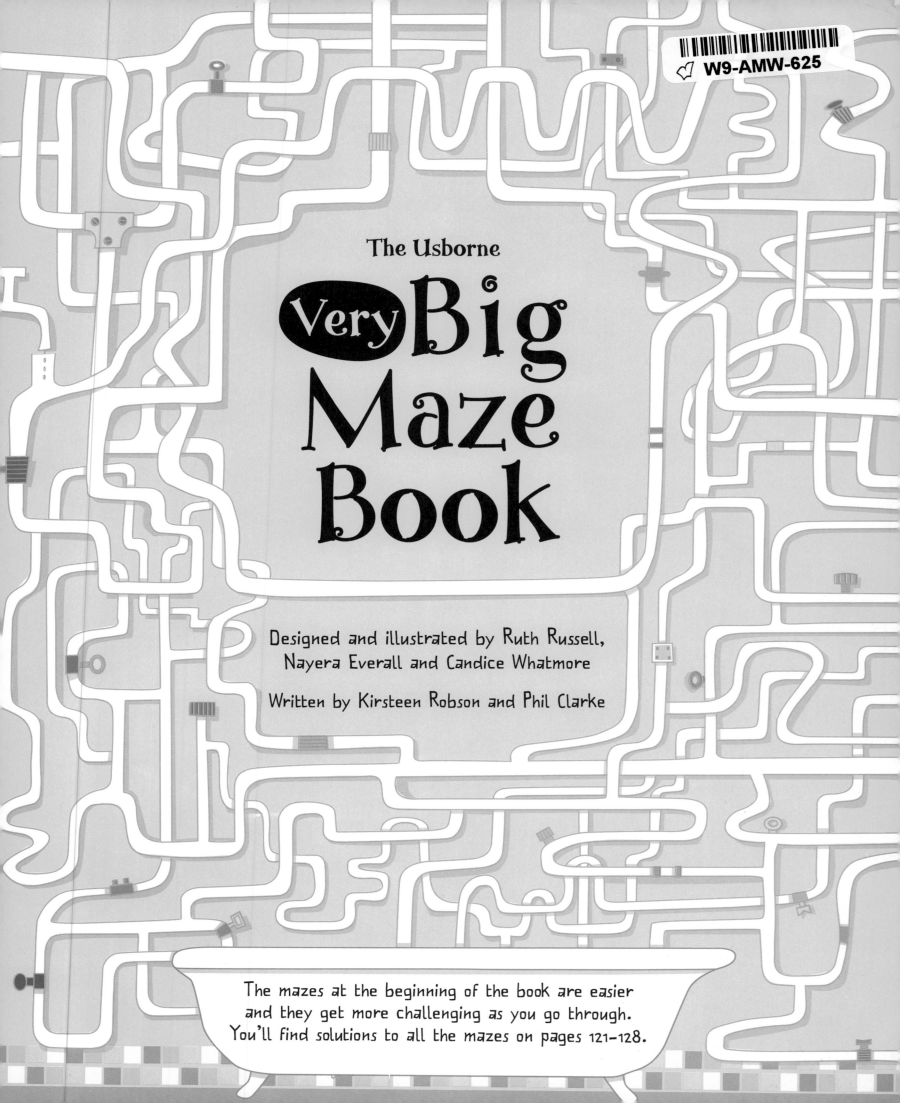

The Usborne

Very Big Maze Book

Designed and illustrated by Ruth Russell,
Nayera Everall and Candice Whatmore

Written by Kirsteen Robson and Phil Clarke

The mazes at the beginning of the book are easier
and they get more challenging as you go through.
You'll find solutions to all the mazes on pages 121–128.

Turtle tangle

Guide Hurtle the turtle through the winding weeds back to his mother.

Hurtle

Mother

All the animals

Every animal in the farm park is worth a look. Can you walk along every single path without going along one twice or crossing your own tracks?

ENTRANCE

WAY OUT →

3

Penguin playtime

Can you help Percy the penguin across the ice field to join his playmates (without getting his flippers wet)?

Percy

Digger dilemma

Dougie needs to drive his digger to the patch marked X to dig a hole. Unfortunately the blue digger has been shifting the heavy rocks around and has made a mess. Which way should Dougie go?

Dougie's digger

Start here

DIG HERE

5

Follow the herd

Help Andy the Alamosaurus find the way back to his herd. Stick to the paths and watch out for hungry green Tyrannosaurs.

Andy

Marina maze

It's time for some summer fun in the sand and sun. Guide the family from the boat to the beach, but don't disturb the fisherman.

Anthill antics

The ants are celebrating spring. Wes the worker ant needs to tell each friend with a leaf to follow him to the Great Hole to prepare for the feast. Which route should he take?

Wes

The Great Hole

Cloudy peril

Guide the plane safely between the clouds to the runway.

Sleds away

Find a clear route down the snowy mountainside to the finish line. You can't go uphill.

START

FINISH

10

Skating search

Find the trail that will lead Monty across the frozen lake to his big sister.

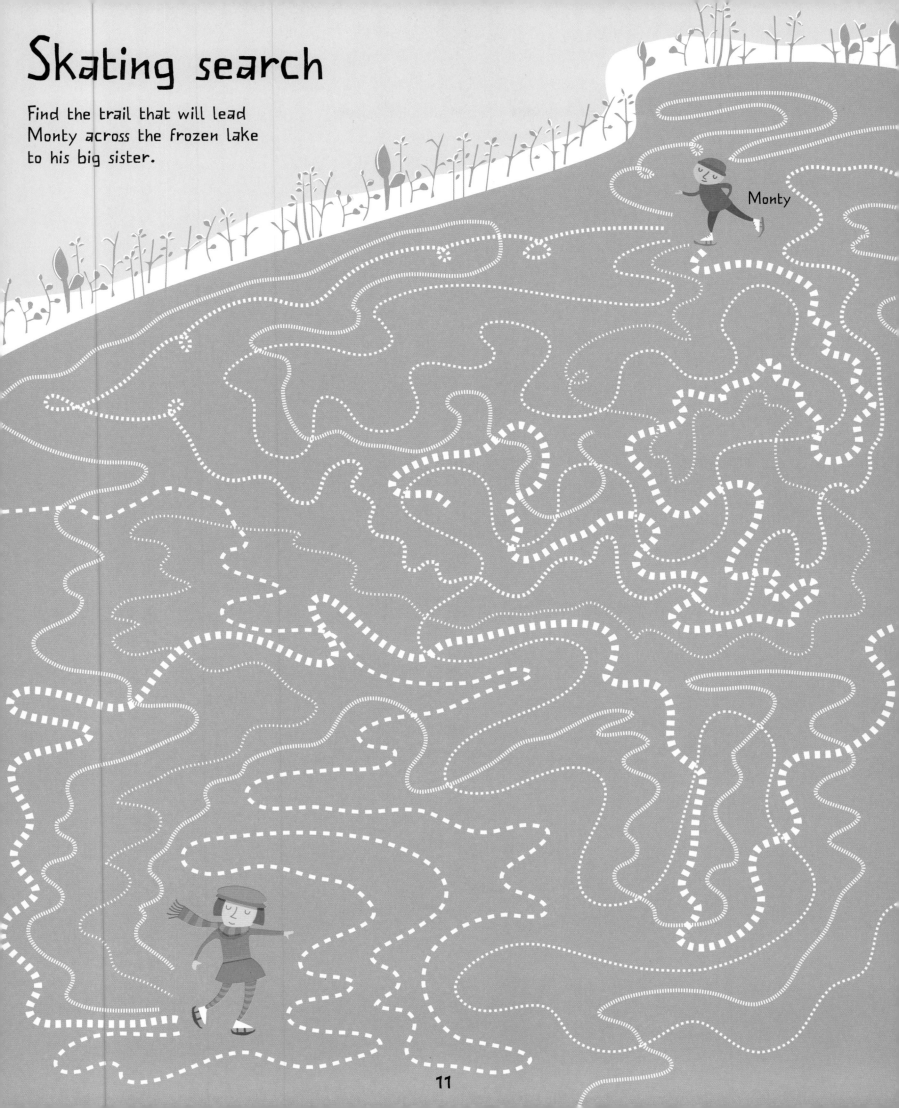

Monty

On safari

Can you plan a safari route to see wildebeests, elephants, giraffes, hippos, lions, leopards, flamingos, zebras, rhinos and crocodiles — in that order? You need to visit every hideout to get a really good view and you can't take the same track twice.

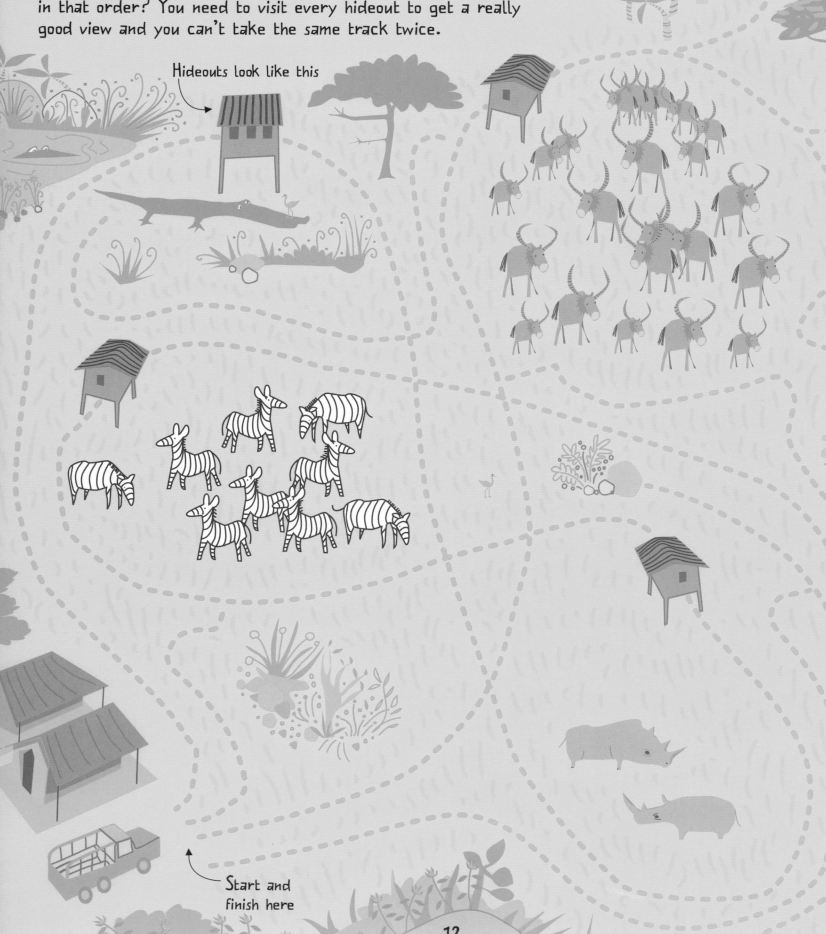

Hideouts look like this

Start and finish here

Graveyard getaway

You need to take a shortcut through the graveyard,
but some paths are blocked by zombies.
Can you make it in one piece?

Finish

Start

Too many tools

Frank has used every tool in his box to fix the car — and now he's feeling hungry. Guide him across his cluttered workshop to his lunchbox for a well-earned snack.

Start

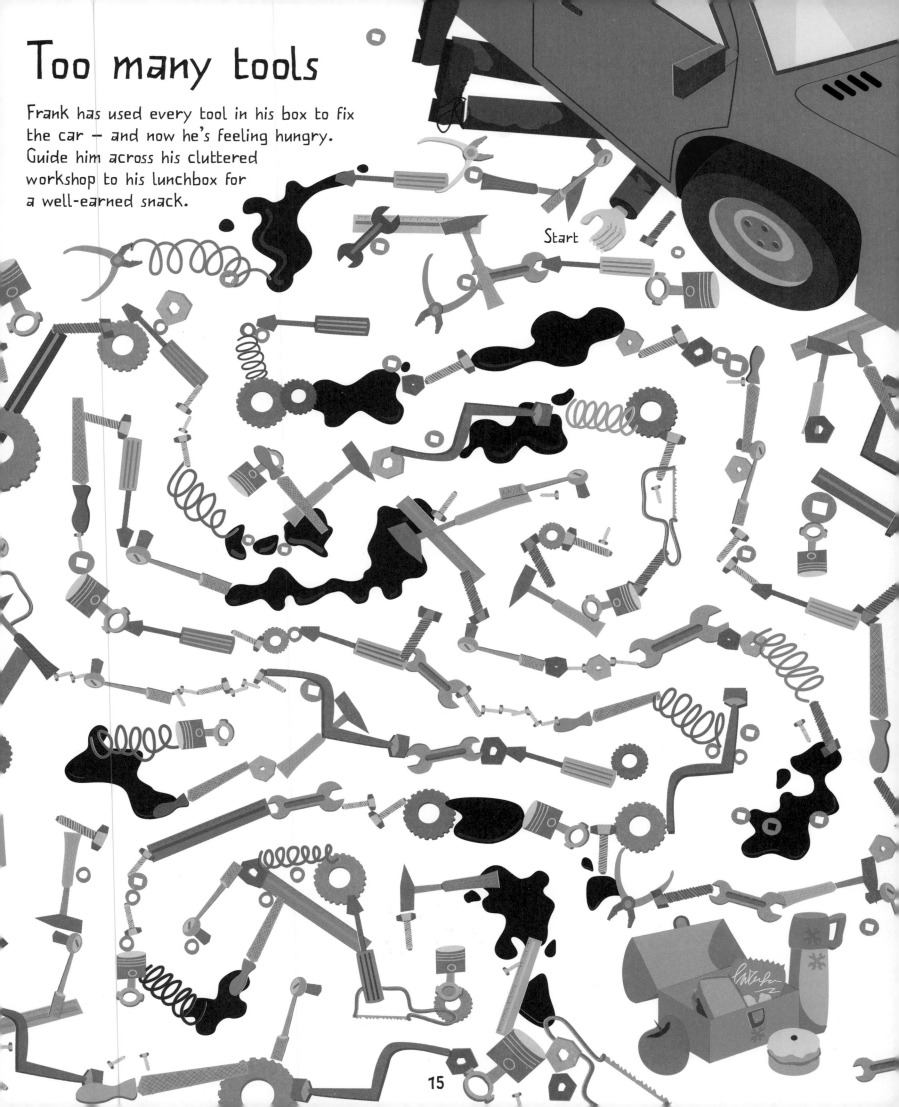

The shelf run

How will the mouse get back to its hole? It can run along a shelf where there's nothing in its way. At the gaps, it can jump across between shelves or down to the shelf below.

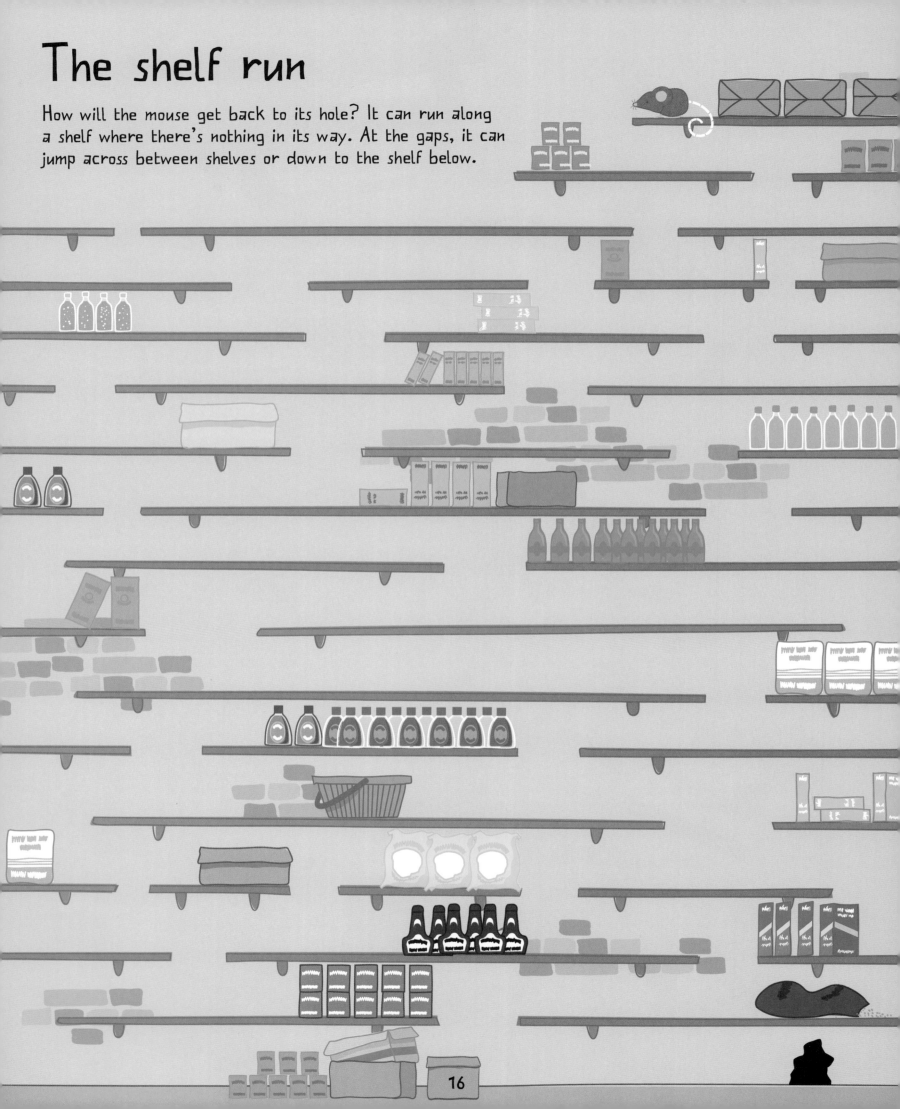

Hidden surprise

Can you help Harry find his surprise
birthday present? How many doorways
will he go through on the way?

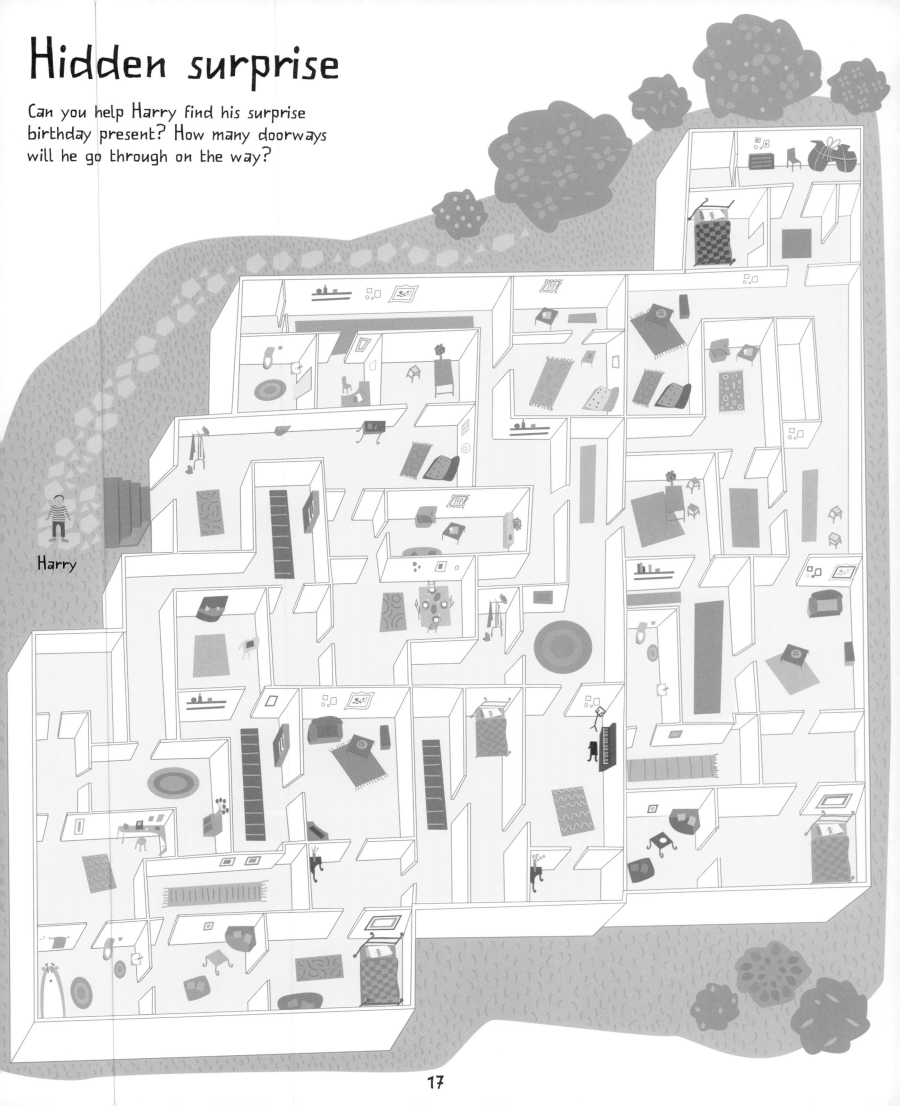

Harry

Busy beach

Vinny has bought ice creams for his parents — but the beach is very crowded and he's not sure where they are. Help him find them without stepping on anyone or anything, or getting his feet wet. His mother is wearing a pink hat and his father has yellow and green trunks.

Vinny

Traffic trouble

Can you find a way to cross the busy road? (Luckily, all the vehicles have stopped.)

Start here

Spiny starfish

Draw a path from the sandy shore to the water's edge without touching any starfish.

Start here

Fred's shed

Find your way through the allotments to
Fred's shed. Keep to the paths and be
careful not to step on any plants
or garden tools.

Start
here

Fred's

Pecking hen

Help Hettie the hen to peck her way along the trail of grain that leads to her house.

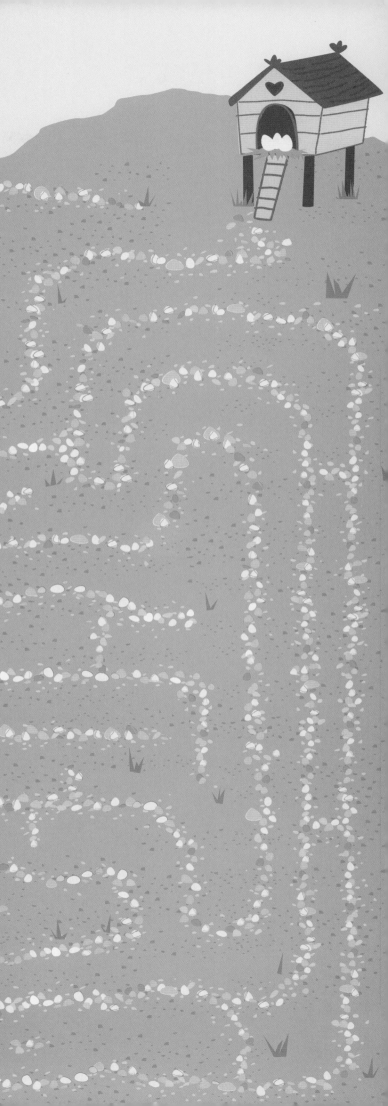

Hettie

Farm visit

Take a trip around the farm, following the activity trail shown on the right. (You may cross a path you've taken, but you can't walk along the same path more than once.)

Start here

Farmhouse

ACTIVITY TRAIL

1. Pick some carrots from the vegetable patch and take them to the ponies in the field
2. Lead one of the ponies to the stable
3. Feed the pigs
4. Feed the sheep
5. Feed the ducks then play on the swings
6. Pick some apples as you walk around the orchard
7. Watch the cows being milked
8. Gather the eggs from the hens and take them to the farmhouse, taking time to stop and look at the wild flowers on the way

Dingle's Pond

Vegetable patch

Lower Meadow

Dingle Dell

The Pink Piggery

The Pony Paddock

Olga's Orchard

The Old Cow Shed

Green Pastures

The Twin Bridges

Sunny Lane Stables

Henhouses

Upper Meadow

Fresh Fields

Rooftop ramble

Camilla needs to get home in time for supper.
Help her find her way along the rooftops to
the only blue house in town. No jumping!

Camilla

Around the underground

Sam and Lucy want to go to the park. Find it on the map and plan their shortest possible route. They can only change to a different line at a circle stop.

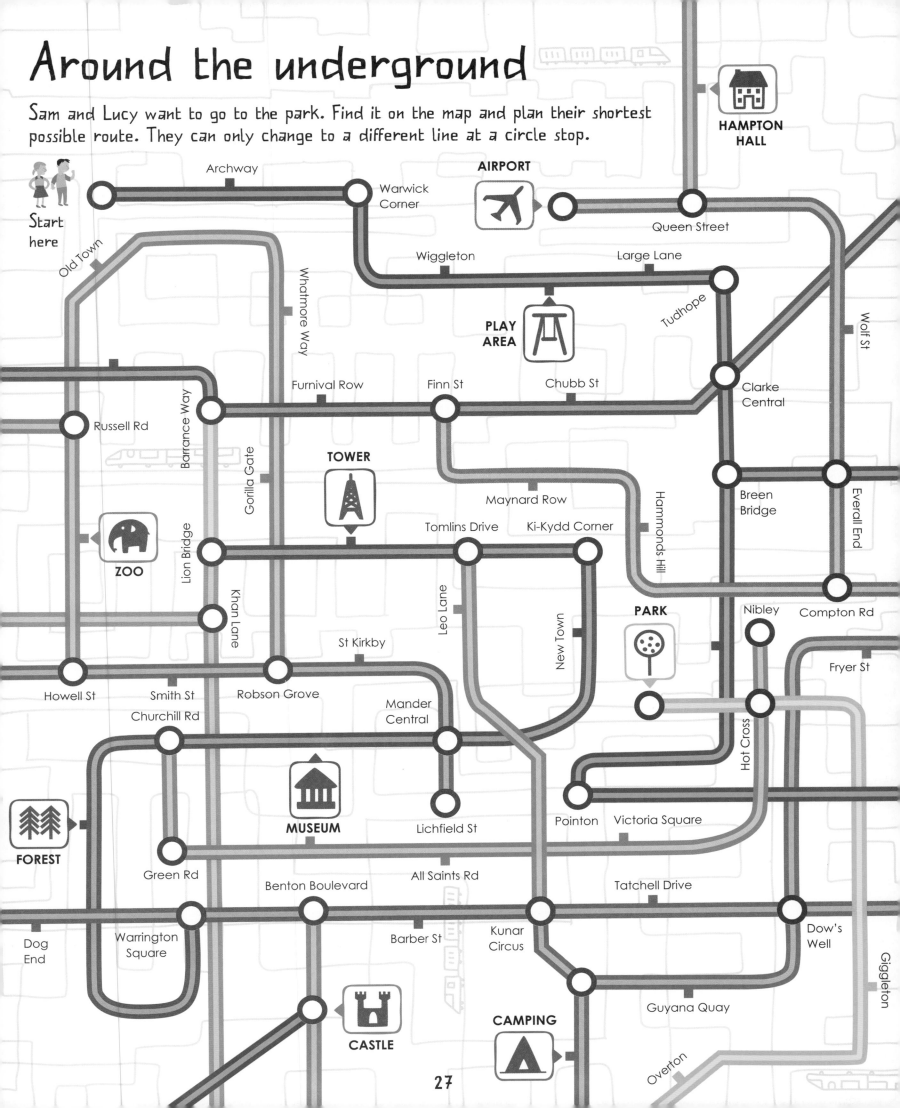

Button match maze

Can you find your way through the maze to another button like this?

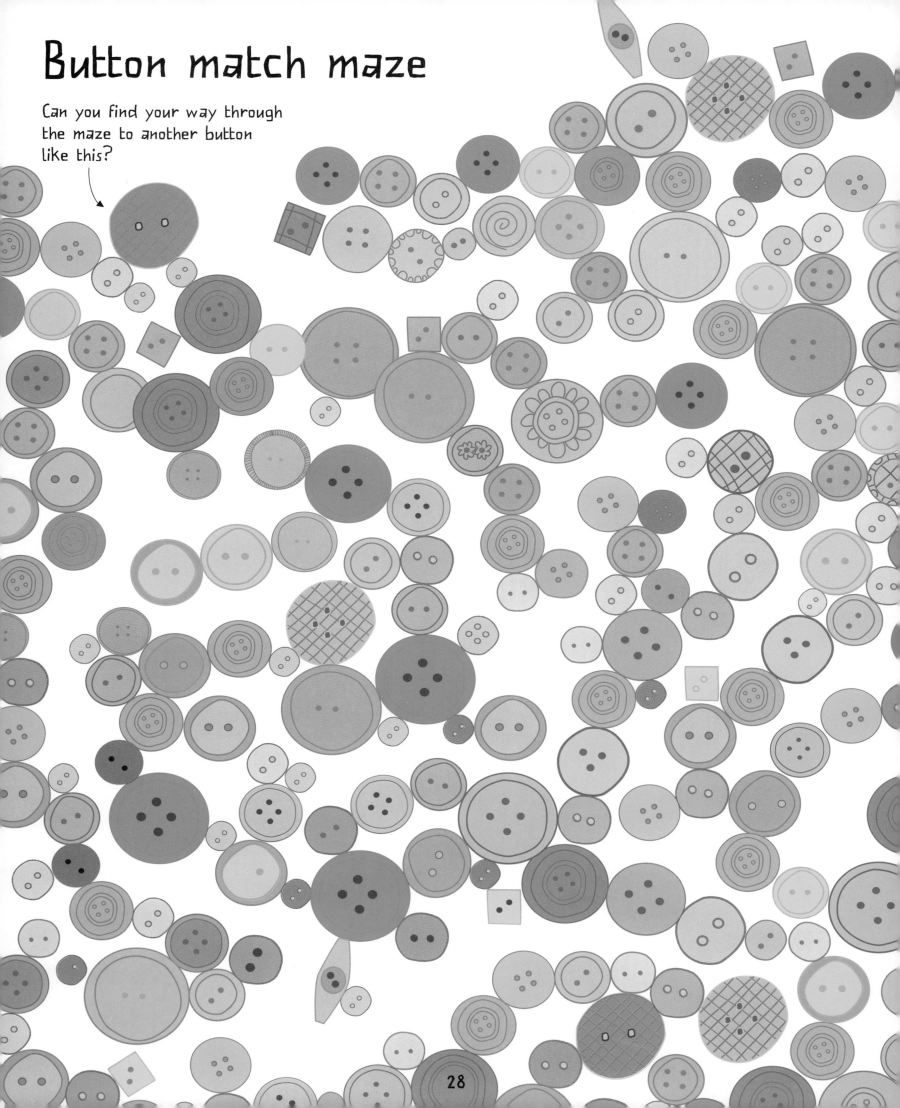

Campsite confusion

The twins have lost their way.
They know they must stick to the
campsite paths — but can you
help them back to their tent?
(Their tent is the only orange
and yellow one on the site.)

Beware of the bears

Find a safe route for the salmon to swim to their breeding waters, avoiding any hungry bears and fearless fishermen that block their way. Waterfalls are not a problem — the salmon can jump up them.

Finish here

30

Start here

31

Biking buddies

Josh is going to meet 12 friends on the way to the park, but he mustn't use the same road twice, or ride on the grass. Which way should he go?

Josh

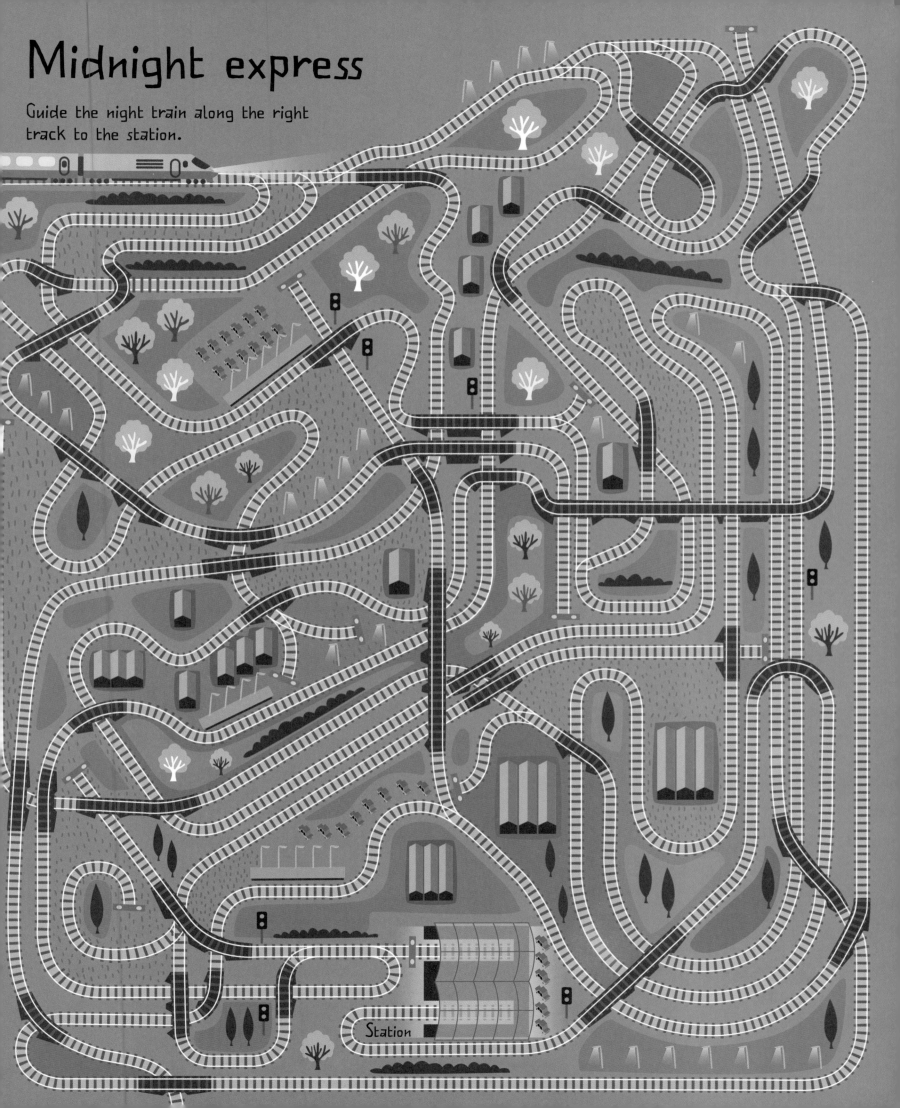

Midnight express

Guide the night train along the right
track to the station.

Station

Loose screws

For a grabber to work, all the screws in its arm must be tight. Circle the only one that can pick up the treasure.

Start here

⊘ This screw is tight

⊙ This screw is loose

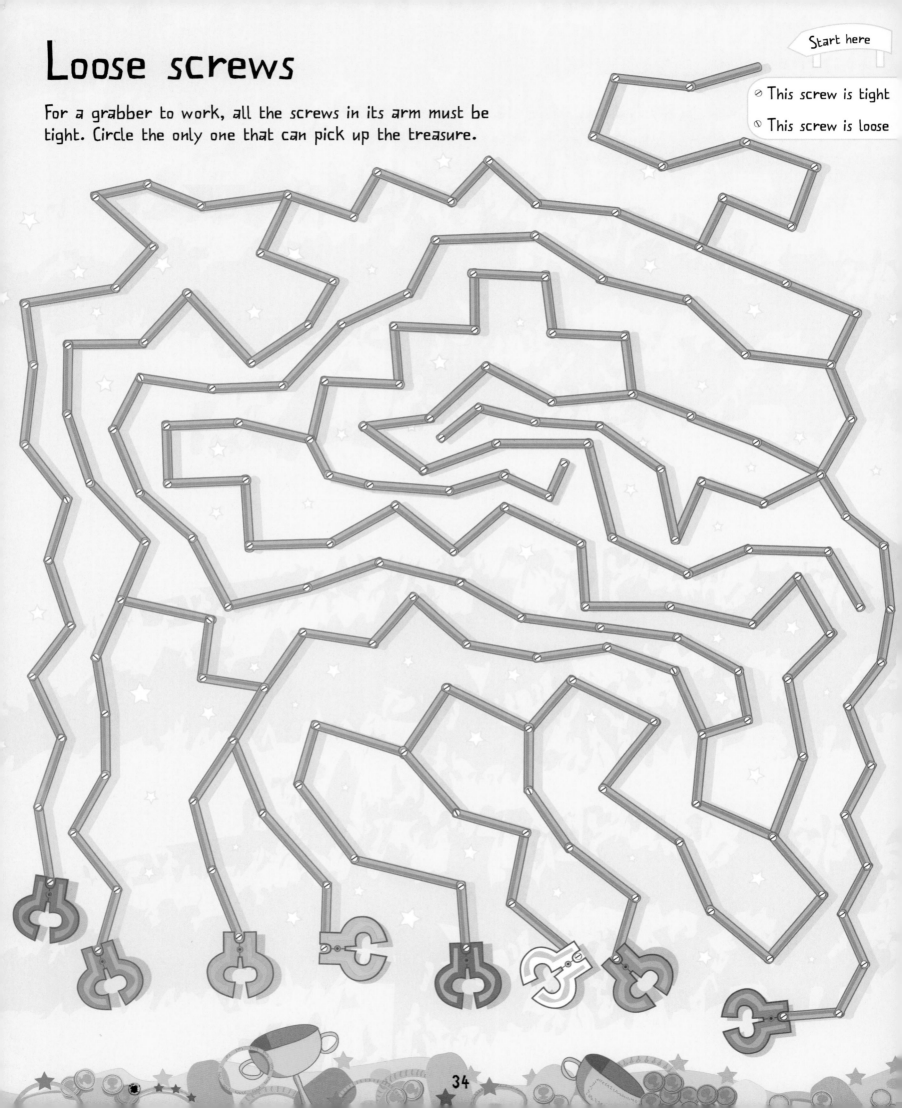

34

Easter eggs

Are you ready for an Easter egg hunt? Find the basket, gather all the eggs without going along the same route twice, then return to the start.

Start here

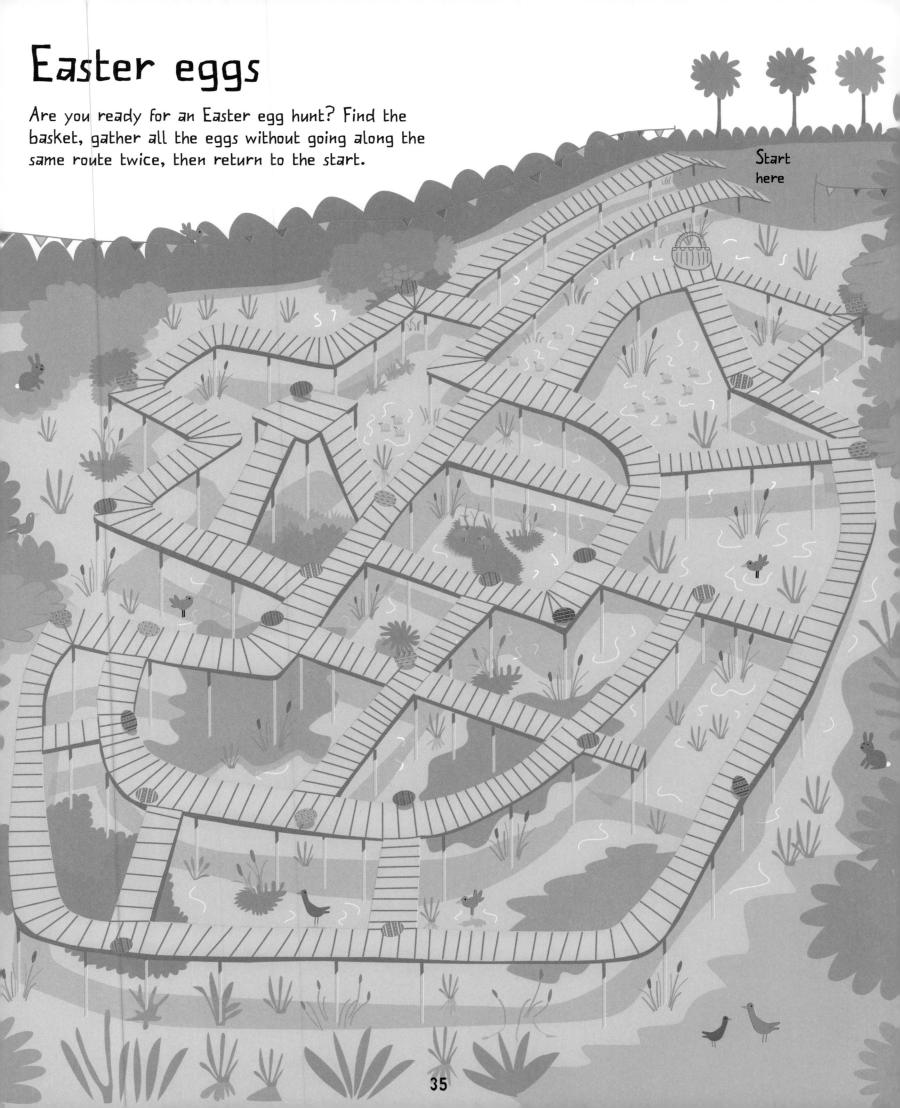

Lost fish

Help Goldie find her brother. She can swim through any gaps where the fish are not touching.

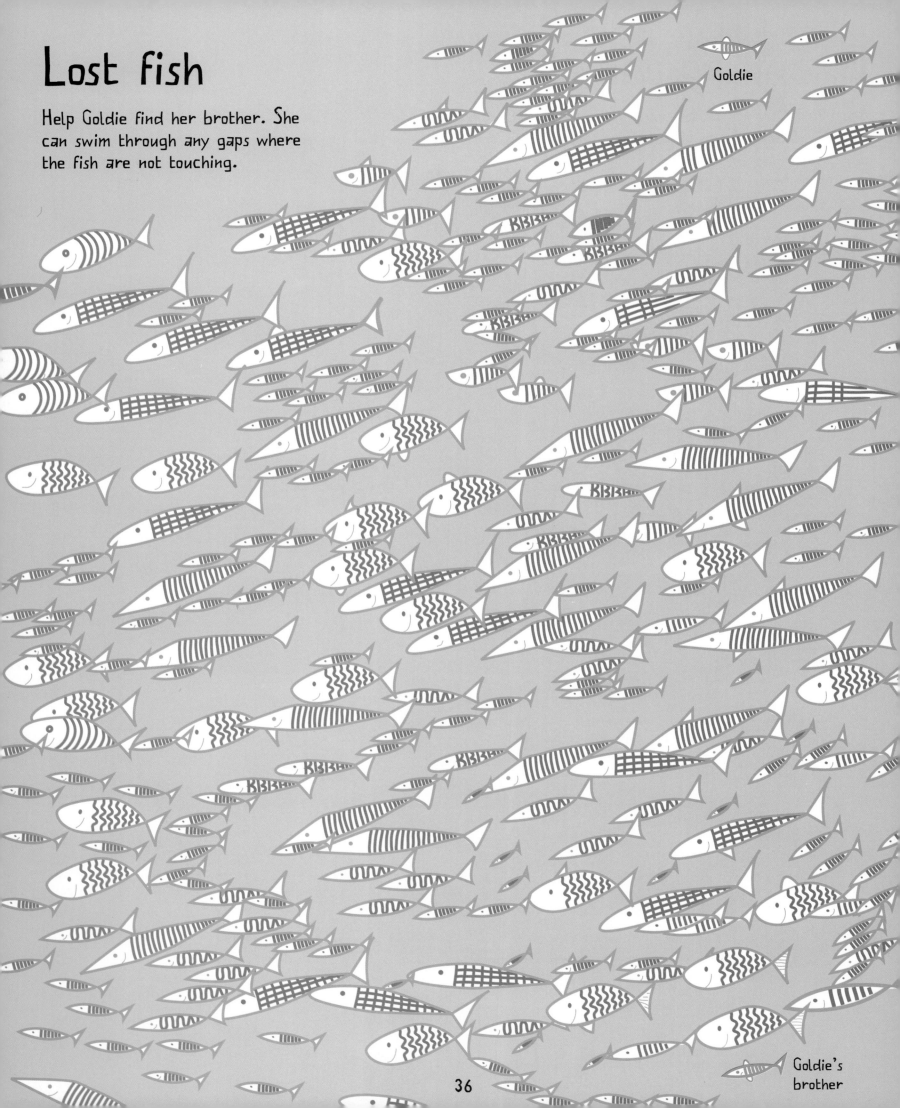

Goldie

Goldie's brother

Walking home

Amy always stops at the swings on the way home from school. Today she also needs to buy a loaf of bread, some flowers, and some toffees on the way back. What's the best route for her to take?

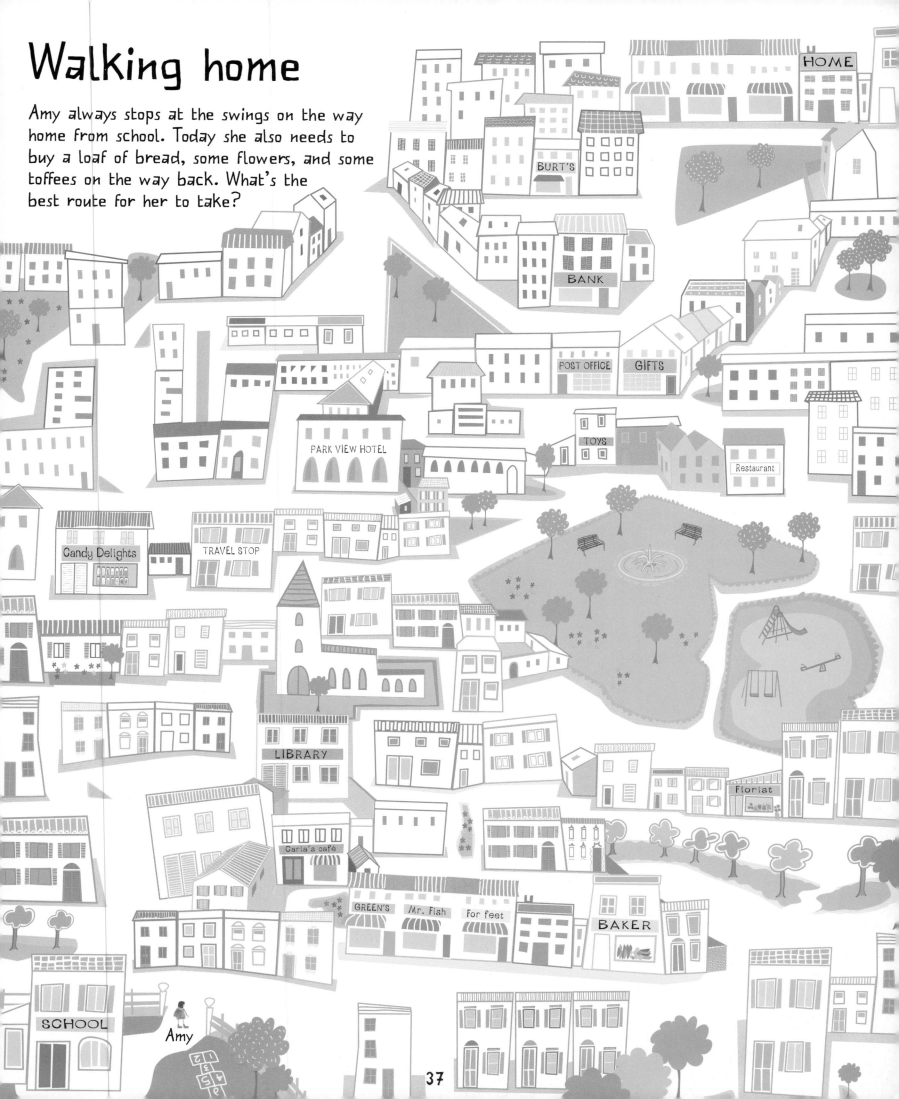

Treasure hunt

Guide Emily through the hedge maze to find
the treasure chest. To open each gate she'll
need to pick up its matching
key along the way.

Emily

Sweet search

Pick your way through all the sweet treats to reach the giant jawbreaker.

Start

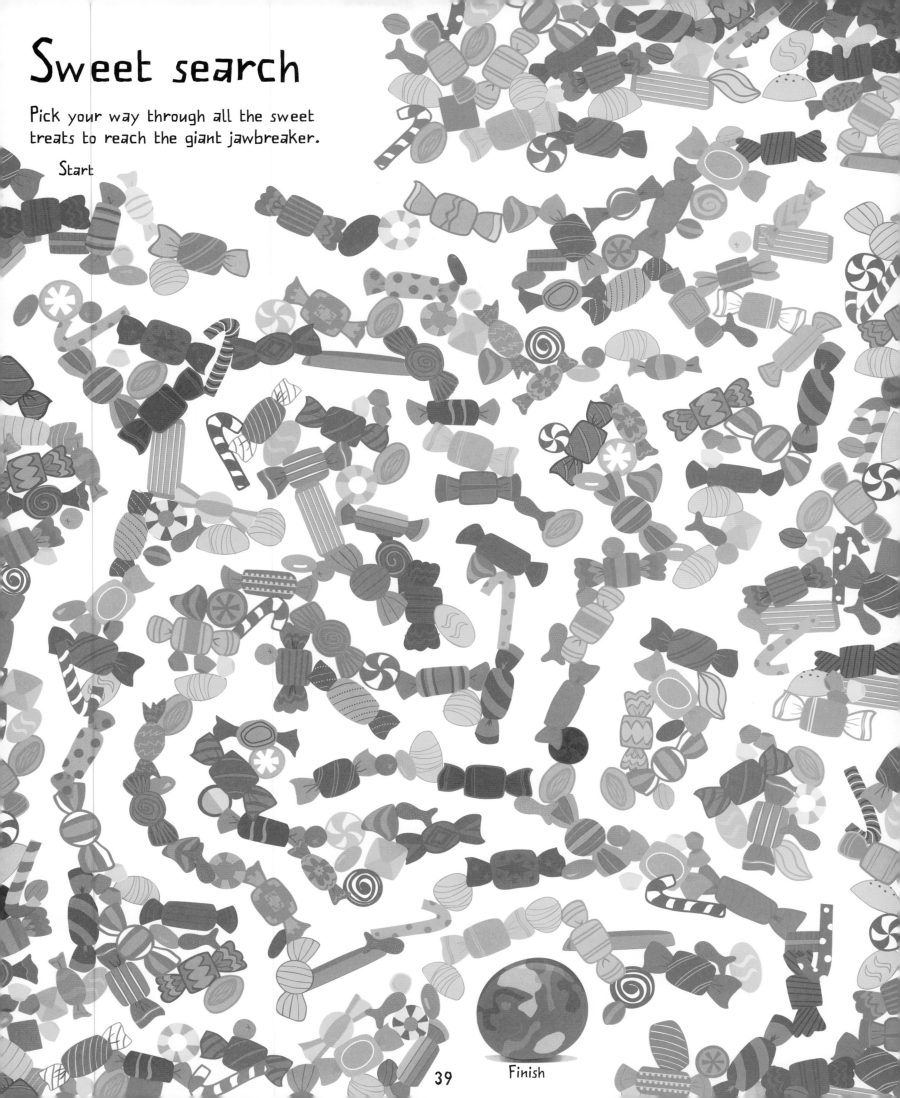

Finish

Sauce and sprinkles

Only one of the buttons on the ice cream sauce machine will work. But can you find out which one?

Feeding flamingos

Florence has spotted a space in the middle of the lake. Can you help her wade her way to it?

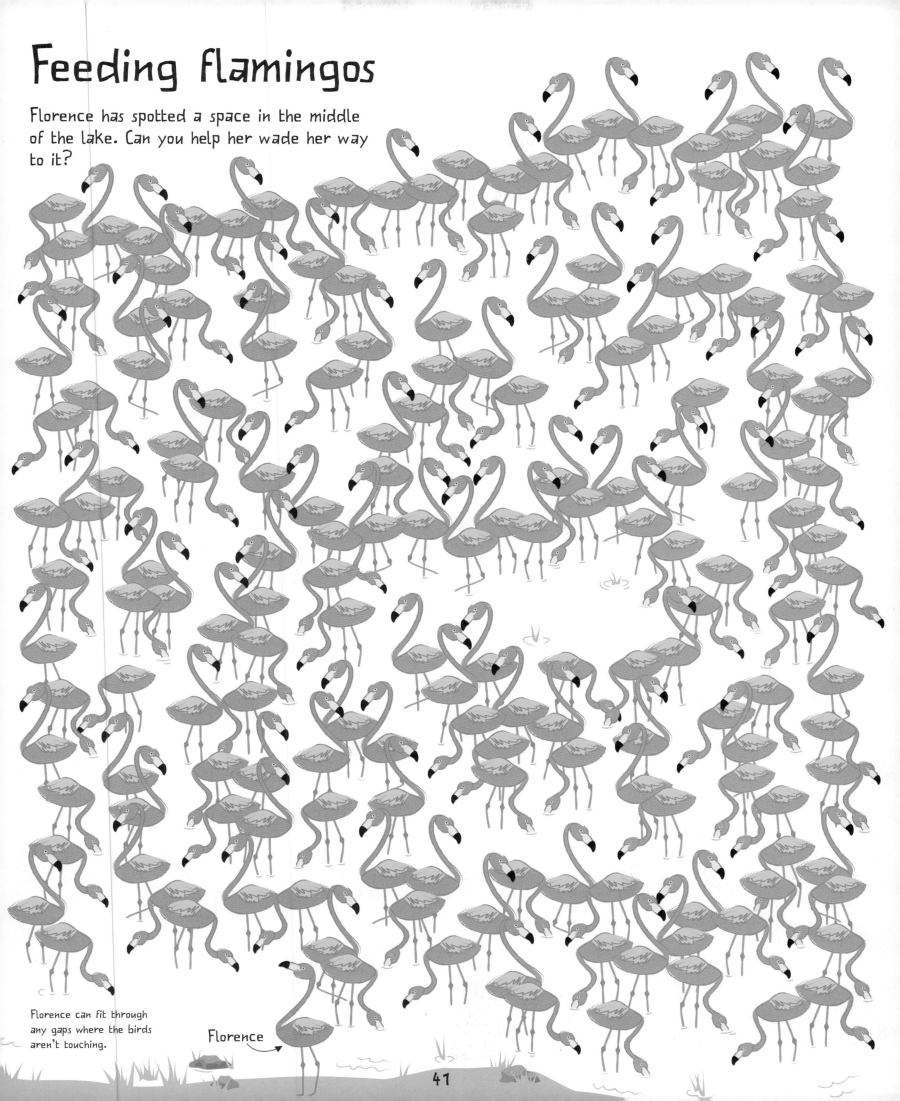

Florence can fit through any gaps where the birds aren't touching.

Florence

Damsel dash

Help the dashing prince reach the damsel
in distress without passing any of the
castle guards along the way.

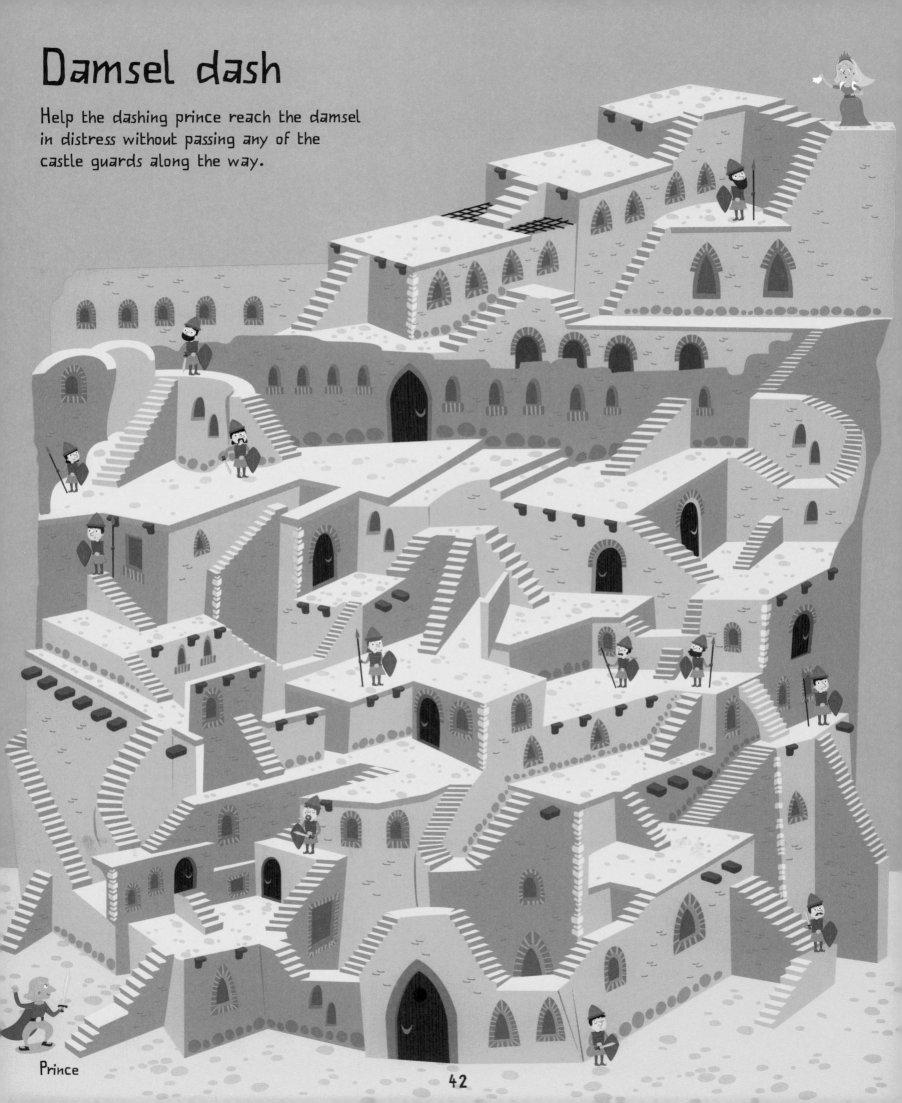

Prince

Hansel and Gretel

Hansel and Gretel know that they scattered exactly
30 white pebbles to lead them safely back to their
father's cottage. Any more (or fewer) than this
may take them to the wrong house.
Help them find their way home.

Hansel and Gretel

Galaxy challenge

Can you help the flying saucer find its way across the galaxy to its home planet, avoiding the star fields and other space obstacles?

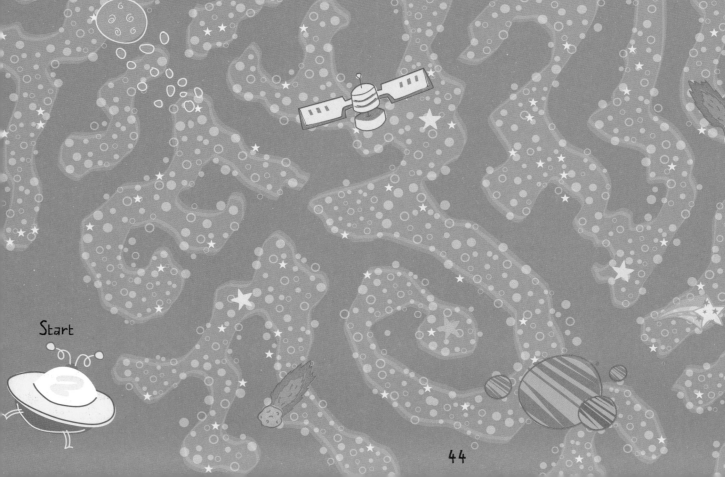

Start

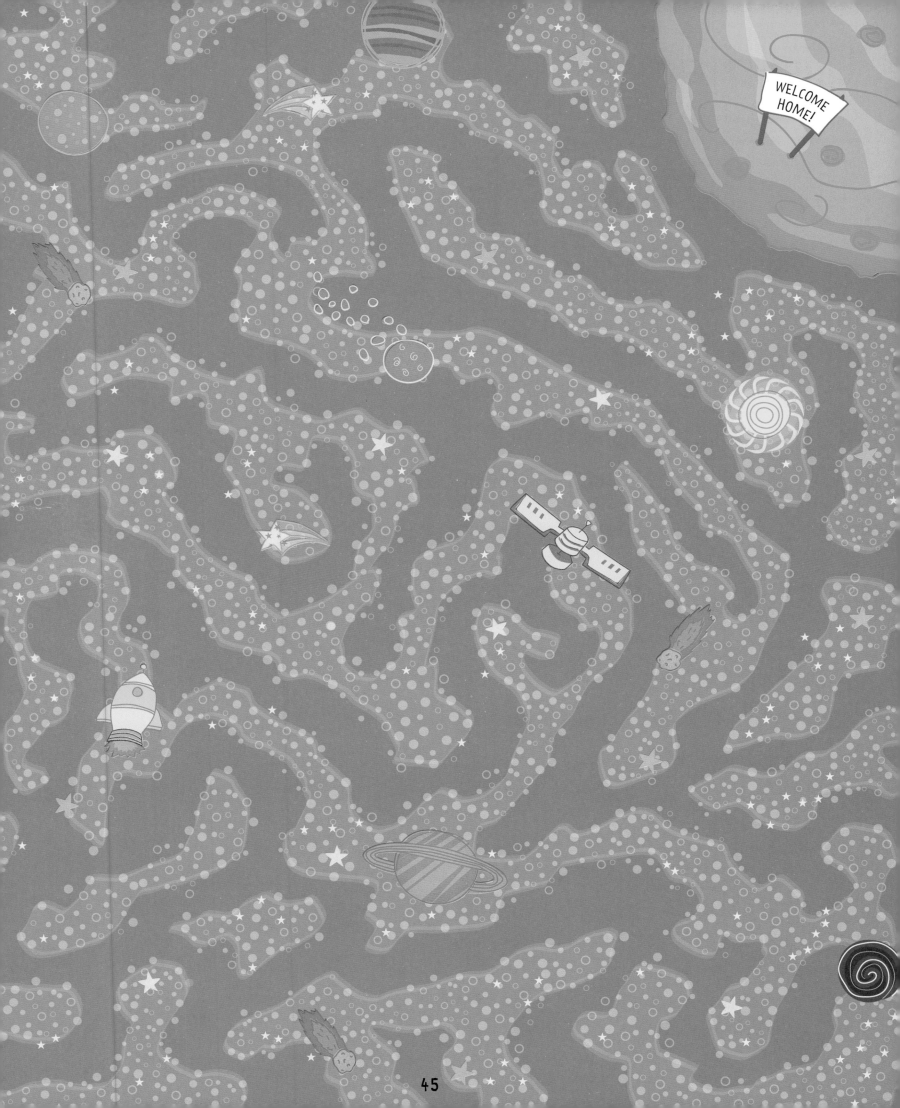

WELCOME HOME!

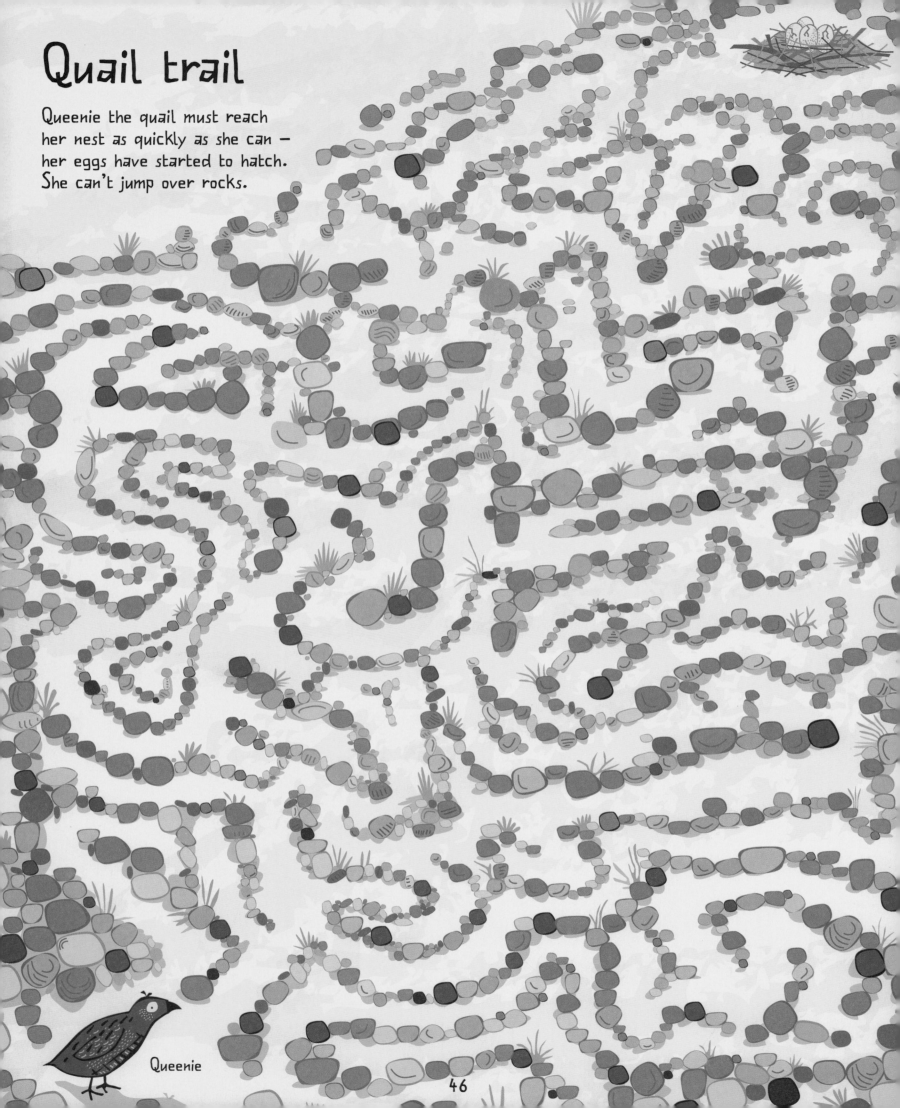

Quail trail

Queenie the quail must reach her nest as quickly as she can — her eggs have started to hatch. She can't jump over rocks.

Queenie

Castle quest

Just one route will take the lost princess and her dog to the Castle of Snowy Canyon. Help her find her way before nightfall.

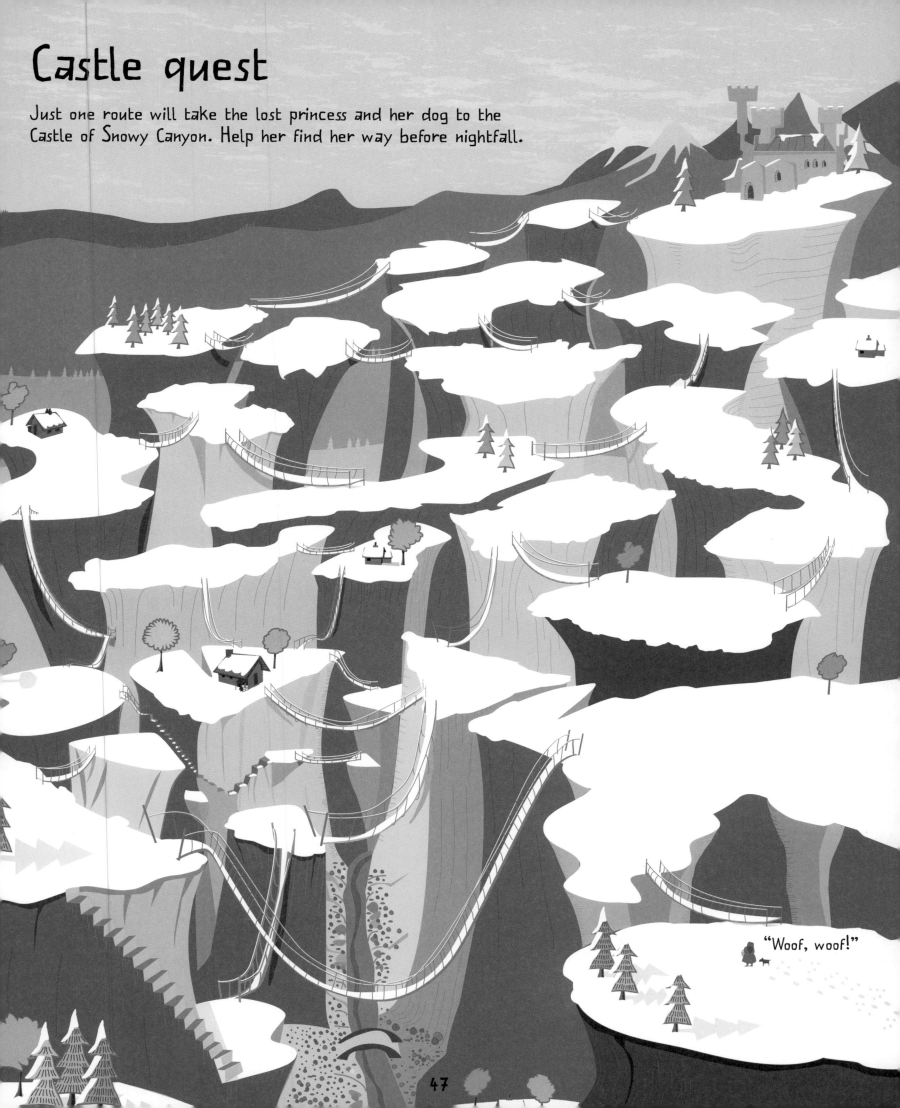

"Woof, woof!"

River rapids

Which way should the canoe go to pass safely through the swirling rapids and continue smoothly down the river?

Vegetable patch puzzle

Help Bobtail the bunny pick a path between the lettuces to the carrot patch. He needs to meet both his bunny friends on the way, but avoid the birds and gardening tools.

Bobtail

Around the airport

A plane is about to land at this bustling airport. Can you guide it safely to Terminal One? Some of the ways are busy or blocked, but there is one clear route for you to use.

TERMINAL 1

Daisy chain tangle

Show how this lonely little bug can squeeze through the spaces to meet its four spotted friends. It can fit through any gaps where the daisies are not touching.

Jellyfish jumble

Help the orange octopus baby swim to its mother.
It can squeeze through the spaces where the
jellyfish don't touch.

53

Snakes and ladders

Make your way from one ladder to the other,
along the snakes. You can only step from a
snake onto another that is touching it.

Start here

End here

Go, Billy goat!

It's feeding time in the meadow, but Billy the goat is at the top of the mountain. Can you help him find his way down?

Billy

Treasure Island

Find the shortest route for the ship to sail safely to the pirate treasure. It cannot sail past islands with skulls on them, and must avoid monster-infested lagoons at all costs.

Pillage Cove

Pointed Peaks

Swamp Island

Scuttle Straits

Land of No Hope

Buccaneer Beach

Cutlass Creek

Dead Man's Island

Treasure Island

At the racetrack

How can the red car win the race? Make sure you steer clear of obstacles and other cars.

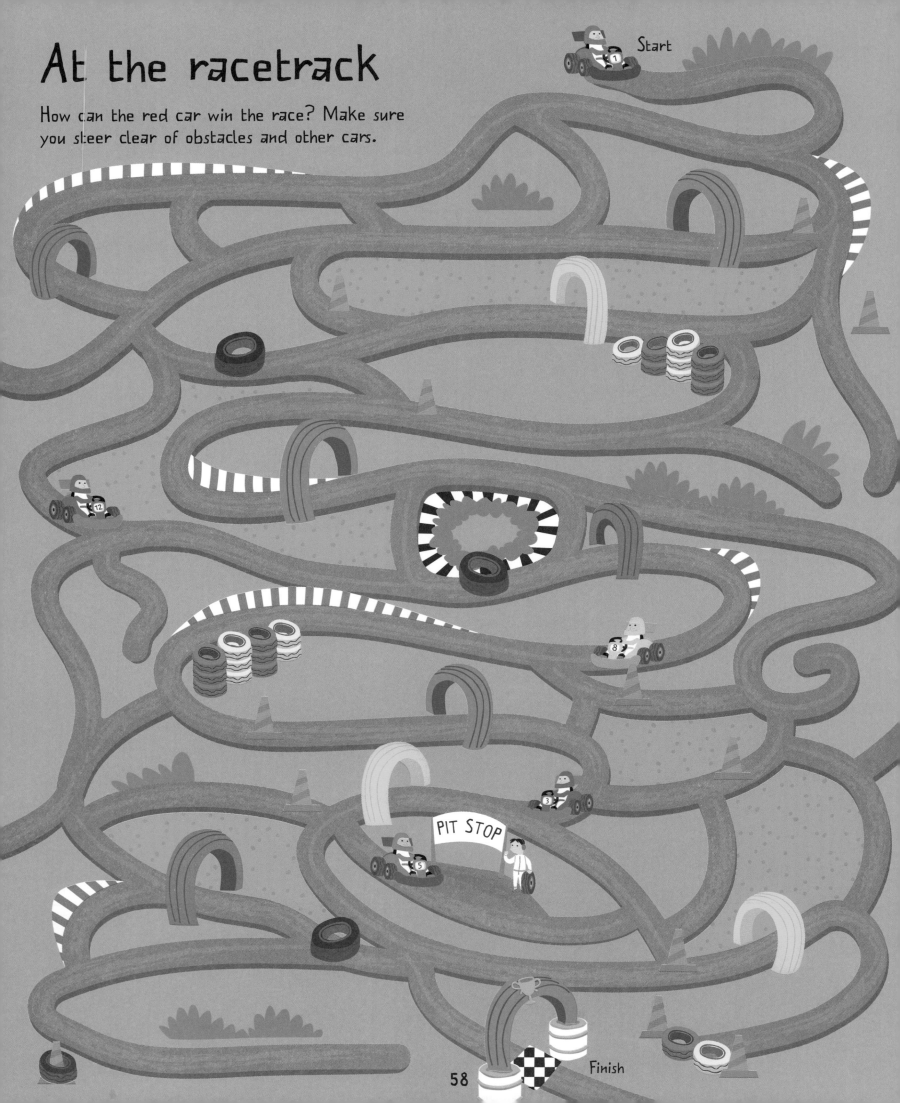

Start

PIT STOP

Finish

Star search

Help Zorg the alien travel to Planet Zing.
He can travel on lines that go through
stars, but not through anything else.

Zorg

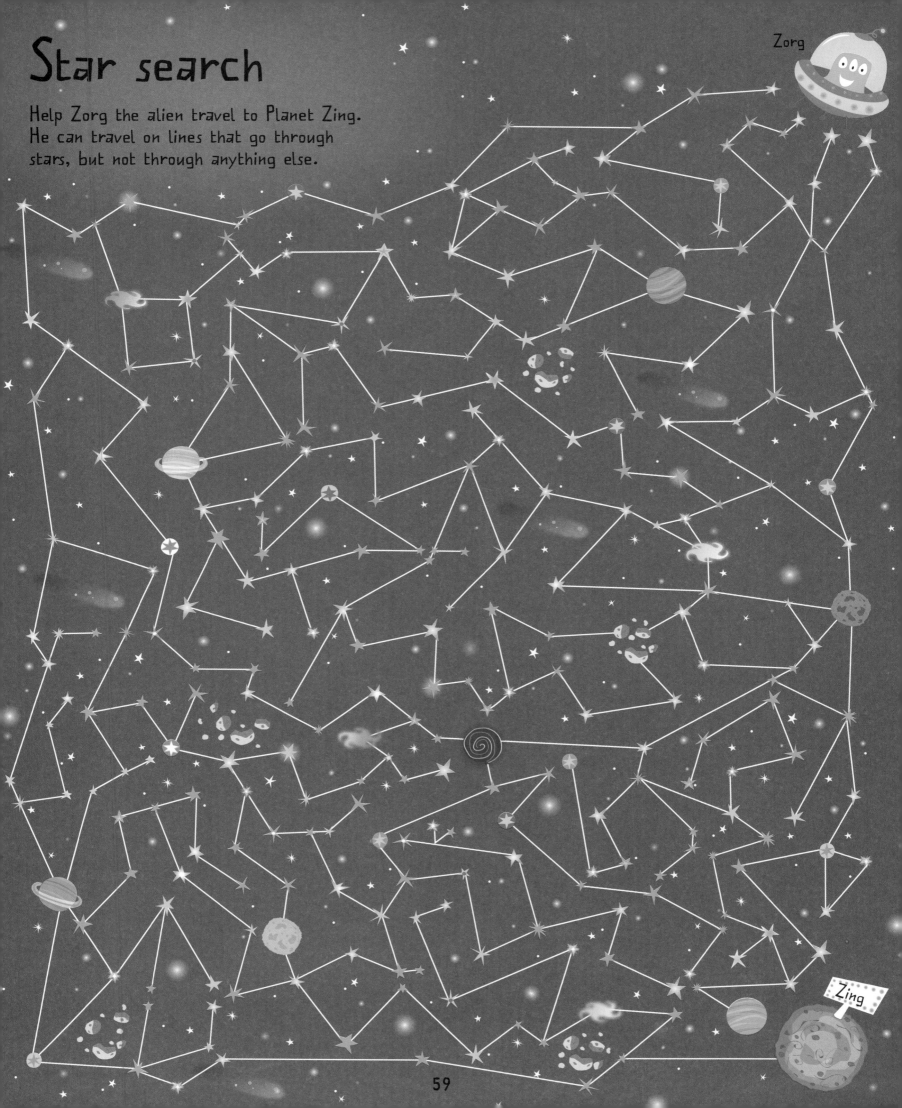

Zing

Chess mess

The chess championship is over and you need to put all the pieces away. But first see if you can lead this green bishop to the other one. You can move it across all four boards, but you are only allowed to move diagonally onto empty white squares.

Bishop

Start here

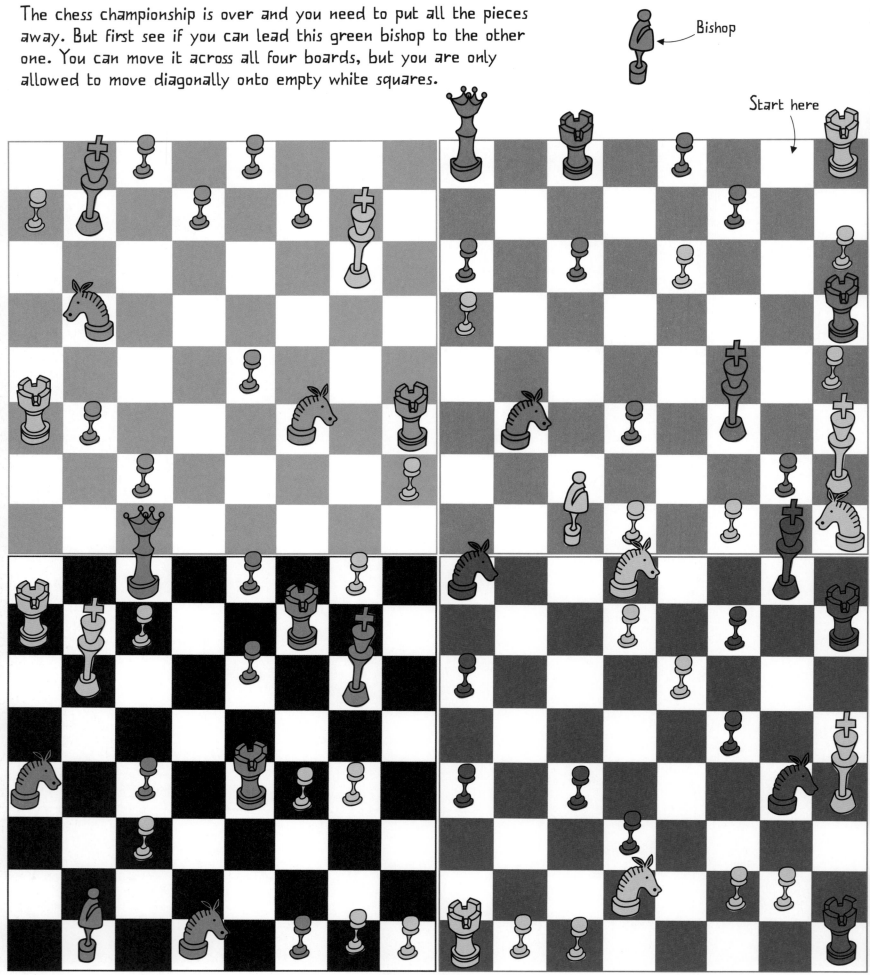

Puzzle planet

Can you help Zub the alien find the quickest
path across the planet back to his spaceship?

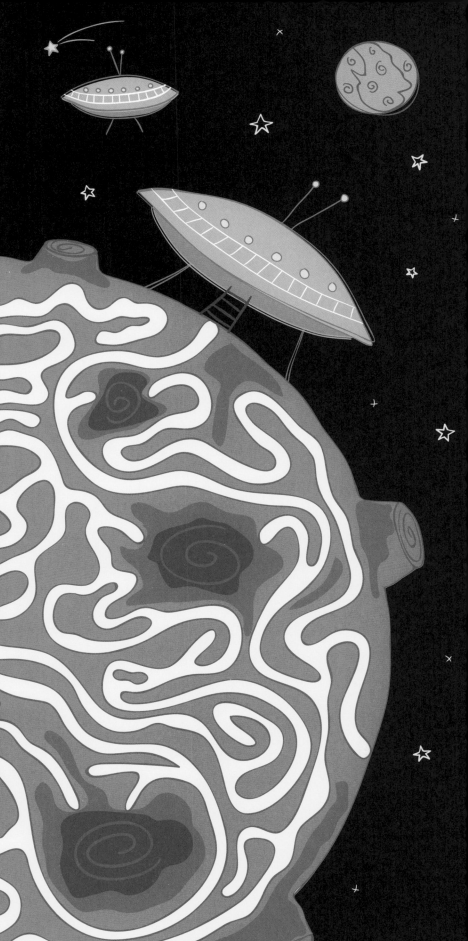

Zub

Milkshake-maker

Find the route the strawberries must pass along to make it into the milkshake.

Toy inspectors

Only the toy with the highest score will make it out of the factory today. Follow the chutes to find out which it will be.

✓ = 2 points
✗ = -1 point

TOYS 4 U

Santa's sleighride

Which swirly smoke trail will lead Santa to a chimney?

Start here

Birds and branches

Which is the shortest route for the baby bird to hop along the branches from the ground to the nest without meeting any other birds?

Start here

Pencil box muddle

The pink pen has lost its top. Draw a path with your pencil so you can reach the top without touching anything on the table.

Start here

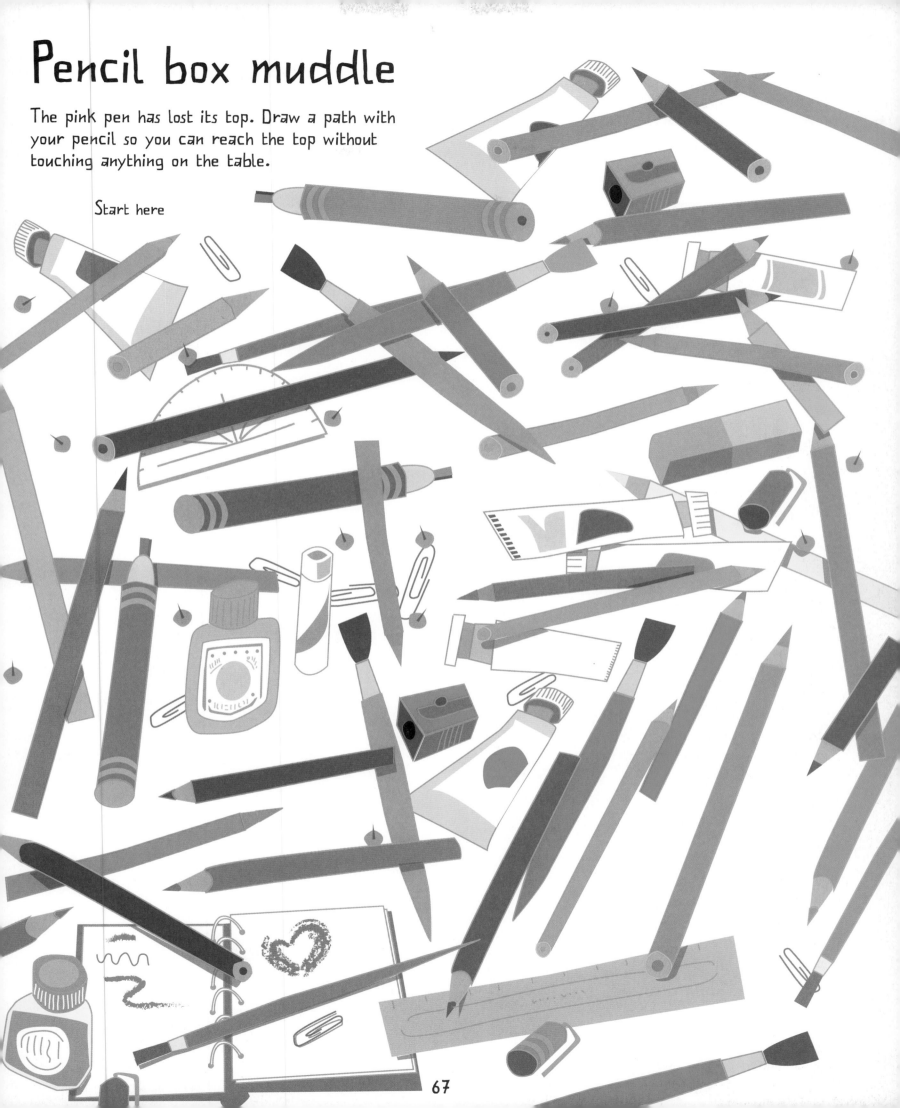

Feed the cows

Drive the red tractor between the fences, avoiding obstacles, to reach the hungry cows.

Hungry cows

69

Flight plan

Which way should Jessie fly to Mazeville?
She can only switch flight-paths at a
fuel stop, and needs the route with
the fewest stops along the way.

● = Fuel stop

The Labyrinth

Find the route that leads the brave hero Theseus to the heart of the Labyrinth, where he hopes to defeat the fierce Minotaur who lurks there. Some passages are blocked by the remains of unlucky adventurers.

Theseus

Lily pad race

Two frogs are going to race to the crown sitting on the giant lily pad. Freddie thinks it's a shorter route across the lily pads, avoiding pale green leaves or leaves with holes in them. Fergus decides to swim between the lily pad paths. Who will win the royal prize?

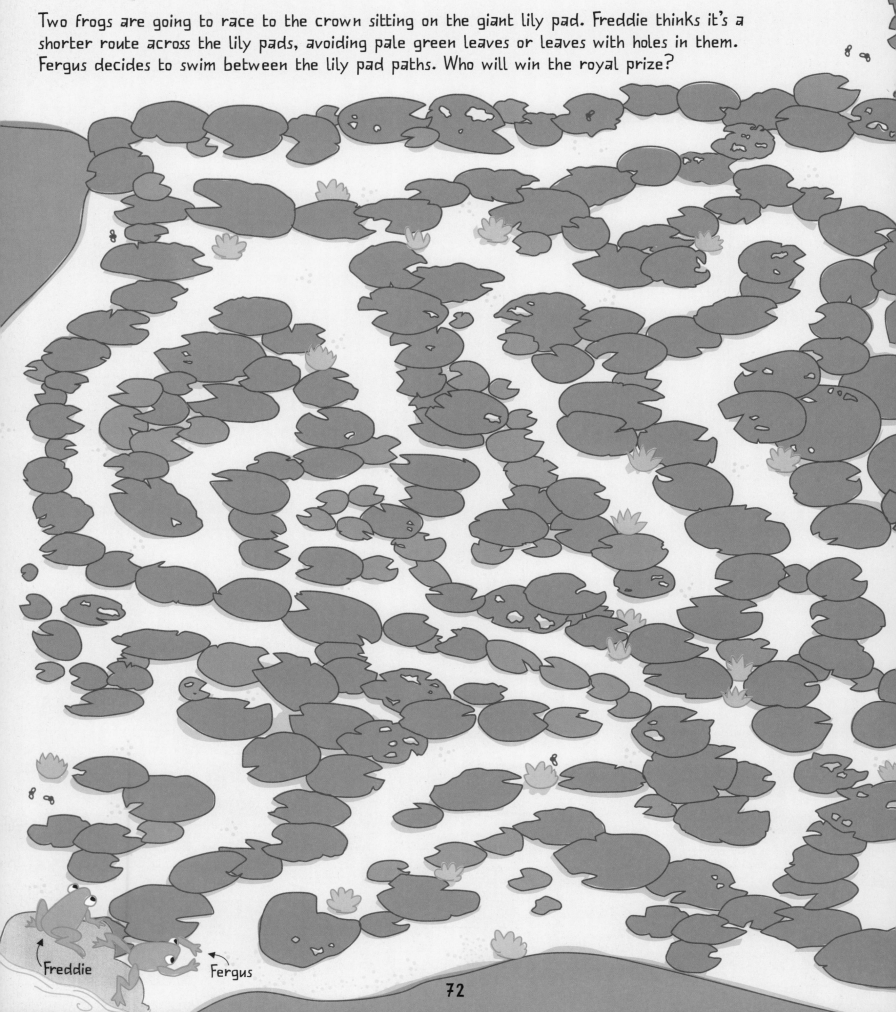

Freddie

Fergus

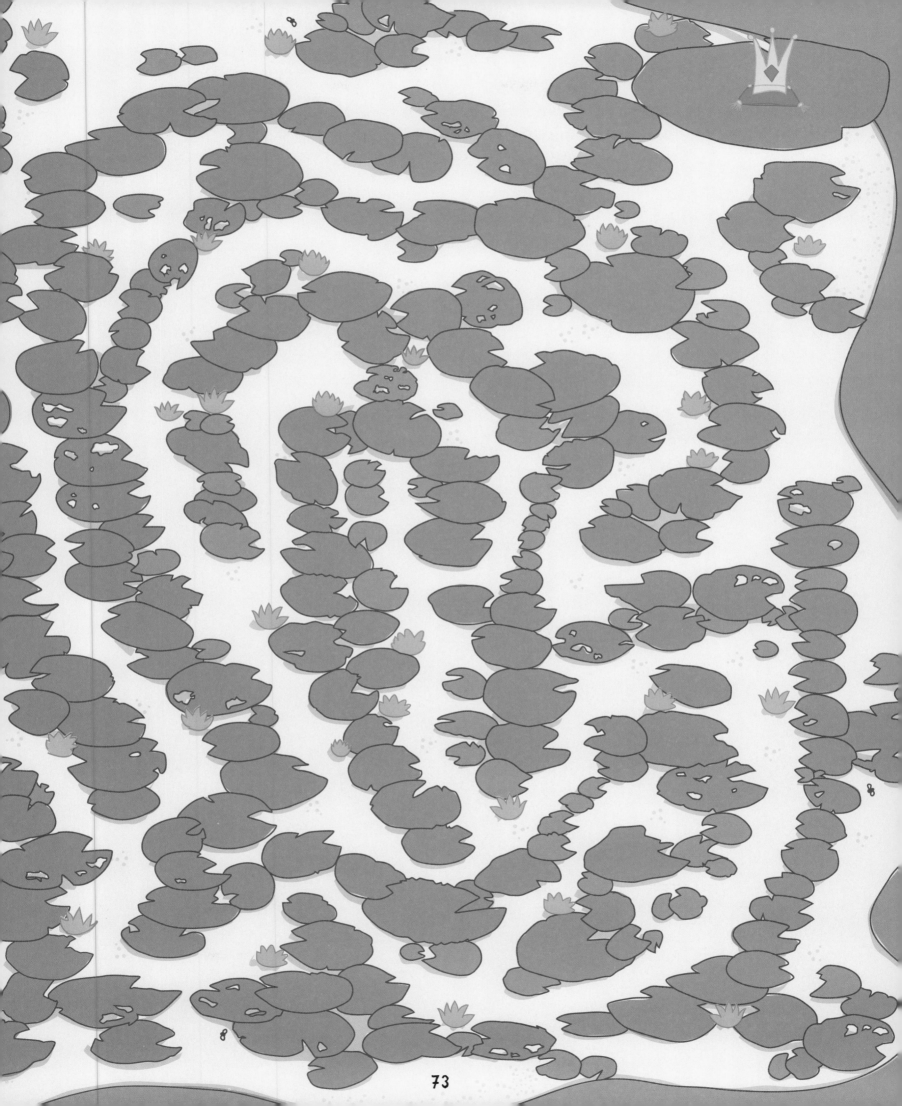

Desert disaster

Oh no! This jeep is lost in the desert. Which track should it take to reach the cooling pool at the oasis as quickly as possible? It can't drive over snakes.

Busy bus

Which is the best route for the bus to drive to the bus station?
It must avoid dead-ends and red no-entry signs.

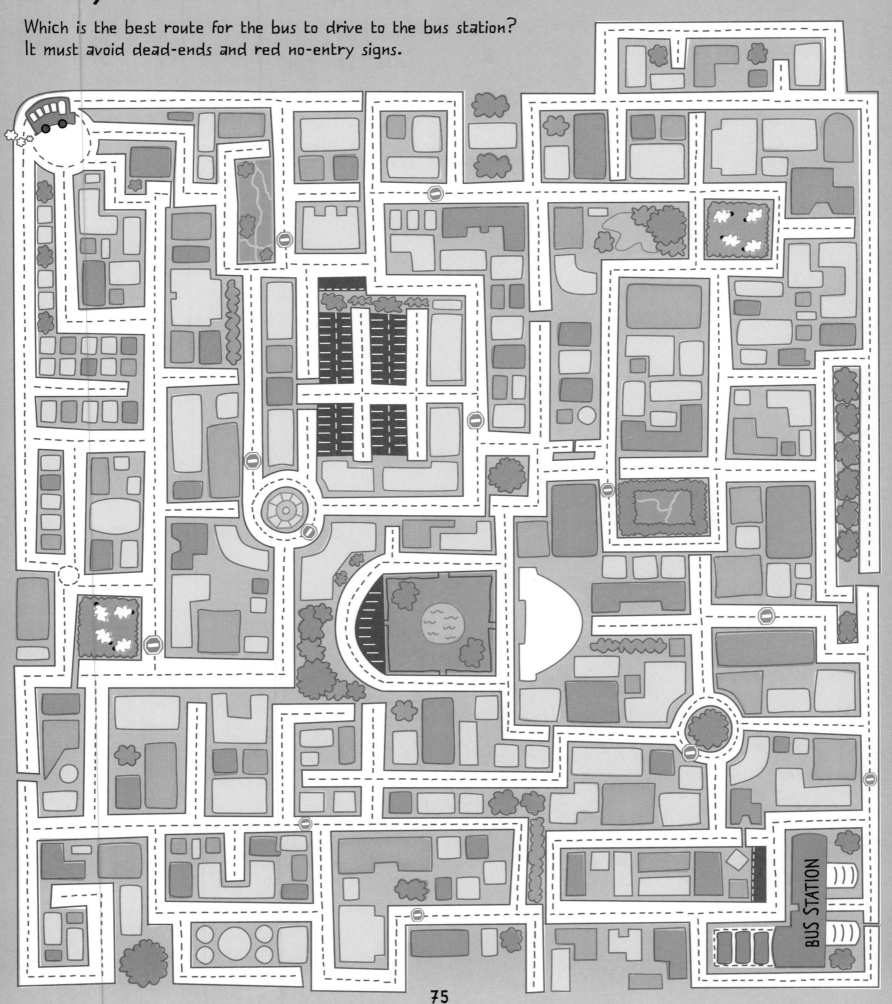

BUS STATION

Bear mountain

Hungry bears are prowling this mountain and it's starting to get dark. But a friendly crow has brought you some advice.

The black house is not safe. Leave it immediately and travel to the white castle as quickly as you can.

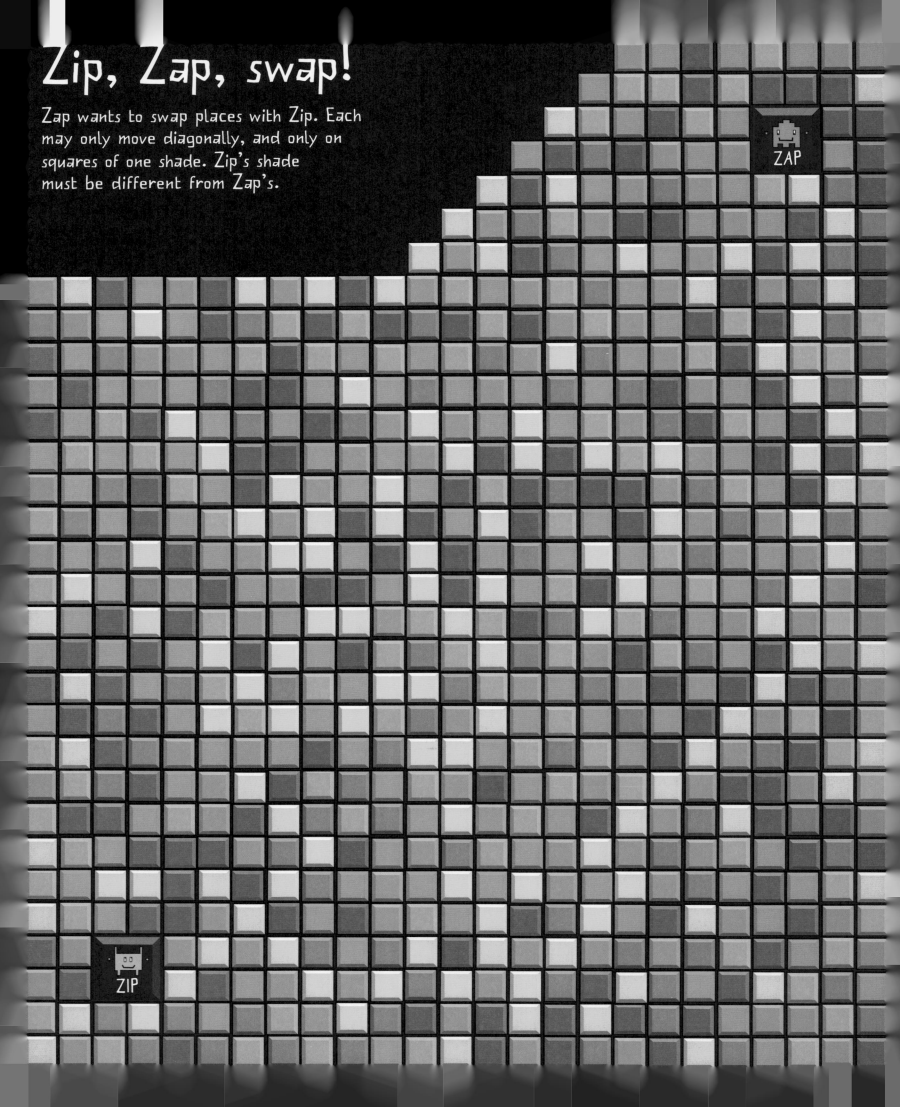

Zip, Zap, swap!

Zap wants to swap places with Zip. Each may only move diagonally, and only on squares of one shade. Zip's shade must be different from Zap's.

Fairground fun

Make the most of your day at the fair by planning a route visiting the Carousel, Ferris Wheel, Log Flume, Ghost House, Blast Off, Tornado Slide, Pirate Ship, Roller Coaster and Biggles Piggles, in that order. Visit the gift shop and grab a burger on the way out. Don't take the same path twice.

LOG FLUME
FEATURING THE 'DRENCH TRENCH'

Mr Munchies

GHOST HOUSE

BLAST OFF

FERRIS WHEEL

Roller COASTER 1

CAROUSEL

BIGGLES PIGGLES

GIFT SHOP

PIRATE SHIP

START FINISH

TORNADO SLIDE

Monkey puzzle

Help the little monkey find its friend.
It can scamper along any jungly vines, but
stepping on a snake would be a big mistake.

Little
monkey

Little
monkey's
friend

Hedgehog hurry

See if you can show the hedgehog family the way to the leaf pile so they can snuggle up warmly for winter.

Camel confusion

Guide the camels through the dunes to the desert market, without being bitten by scorpions.

Market

Eye in the sky

Help the helicopter pilot lead the fire truck along the quickest route to the burning house, while avoiding the tractors and other obstacles.

A walk in the park

Ellie is going to meet her friend at the fountain then visit each part of the park marked with a flag. Help her do it without walking through the same place twice or stepping on the grass. She needs to finish back at the park entrance.

Ellie

Route race

The car that crosses over (but not under) the most bridges will reach the railway bridge first. Which car will it be?

Super slalom

Help the skier complete his time trial by following the route that passes the green, orange and red flags but avoids the purple and blue flags.

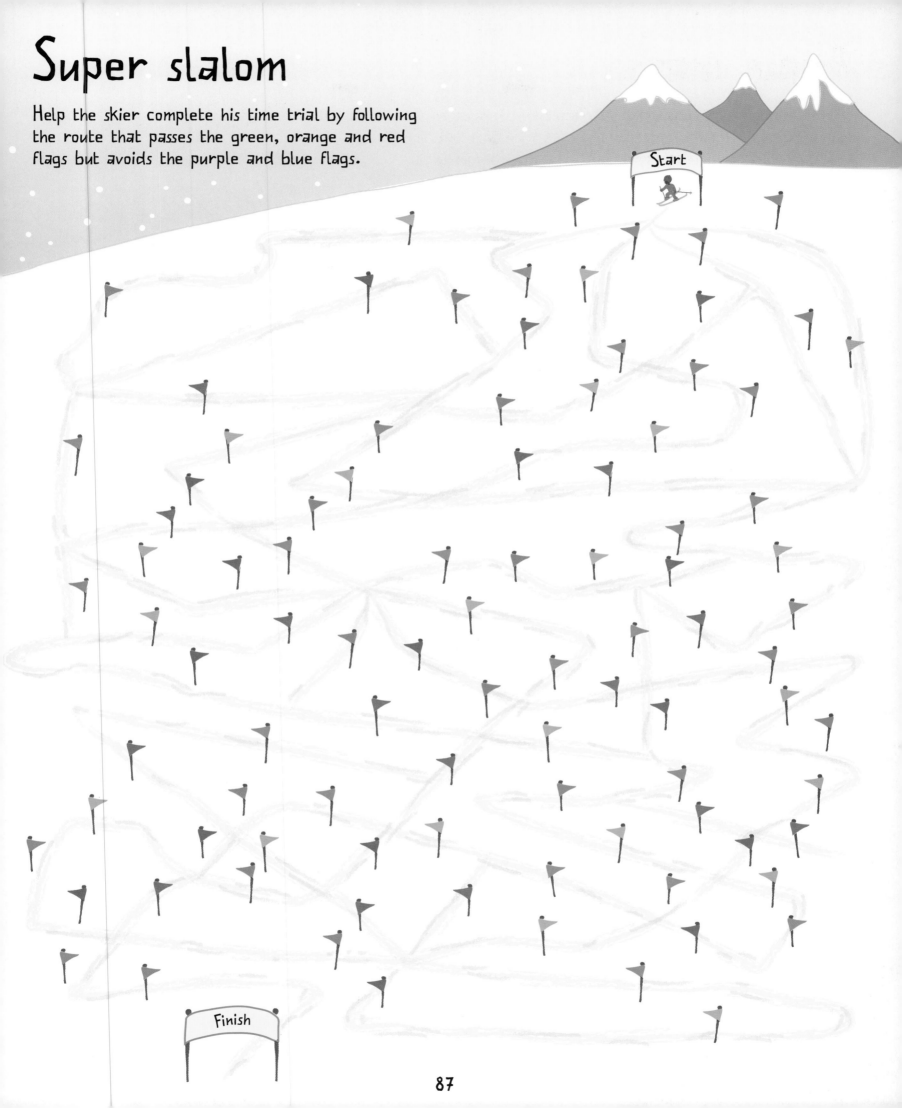

Start

Finish

Apple maze

There's not much of this apple left to munch, but there are still some tasty seeds in the core. Which tunnels should Colin and Caspar take to reach them and who will win the race?

Colin

Caspar

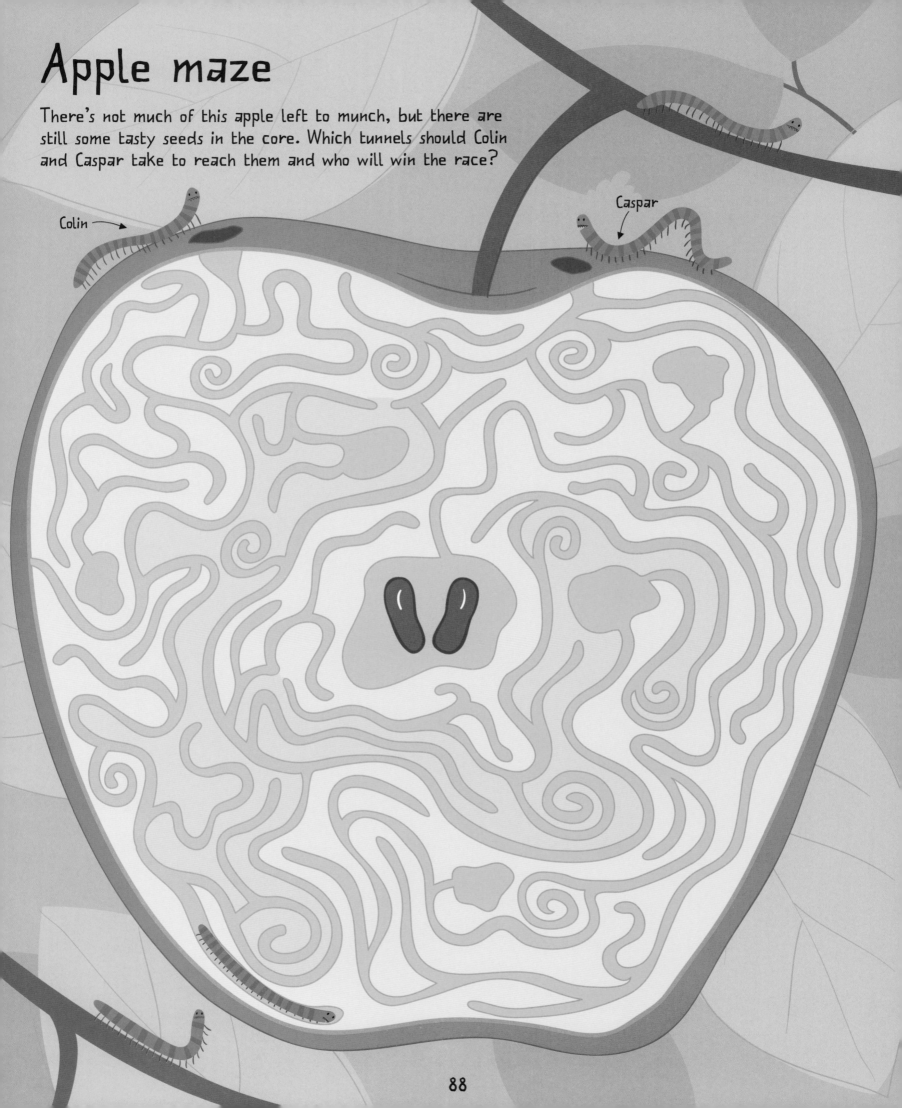

Construction chaos

Find a way for Brian to reach the cab of the crane. He can swing around upright scaffolding poles, but can't get past brick walls or "Do not enter" signs, and he can only go up and down the scaffolding with a ladder.

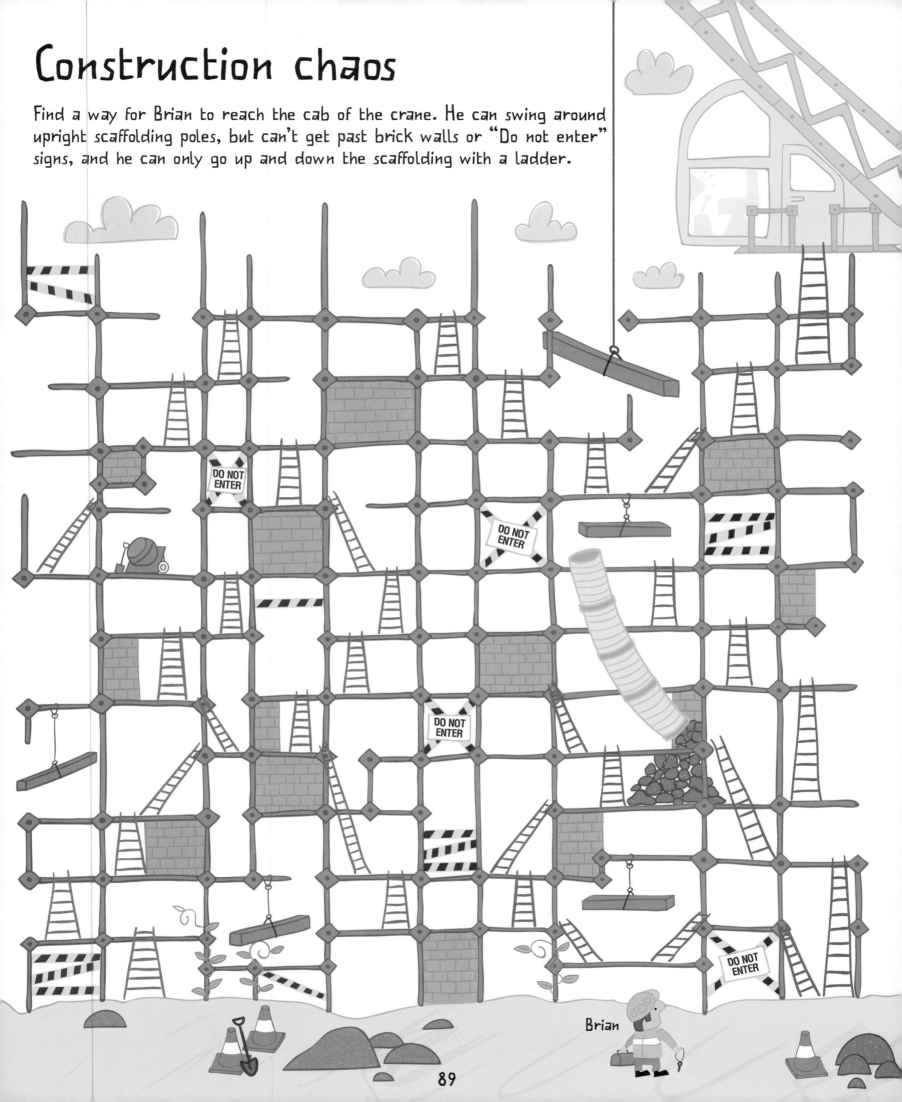

89

Hungry hamster

Henry the hamster is hungry. Help him find the food, without squeezing past the other hamsters.

Henry

Food

Treetop tea party

Help Doris the squirrel deliver her party invitations and return to the ground. She has to visit a friend in each treehouse, but can't use any section of a ladder more than once.

Start here

Peaks and valleys

Help the tourists wind their way between the mountain peaks to the Ramblers' Retreat at the top.

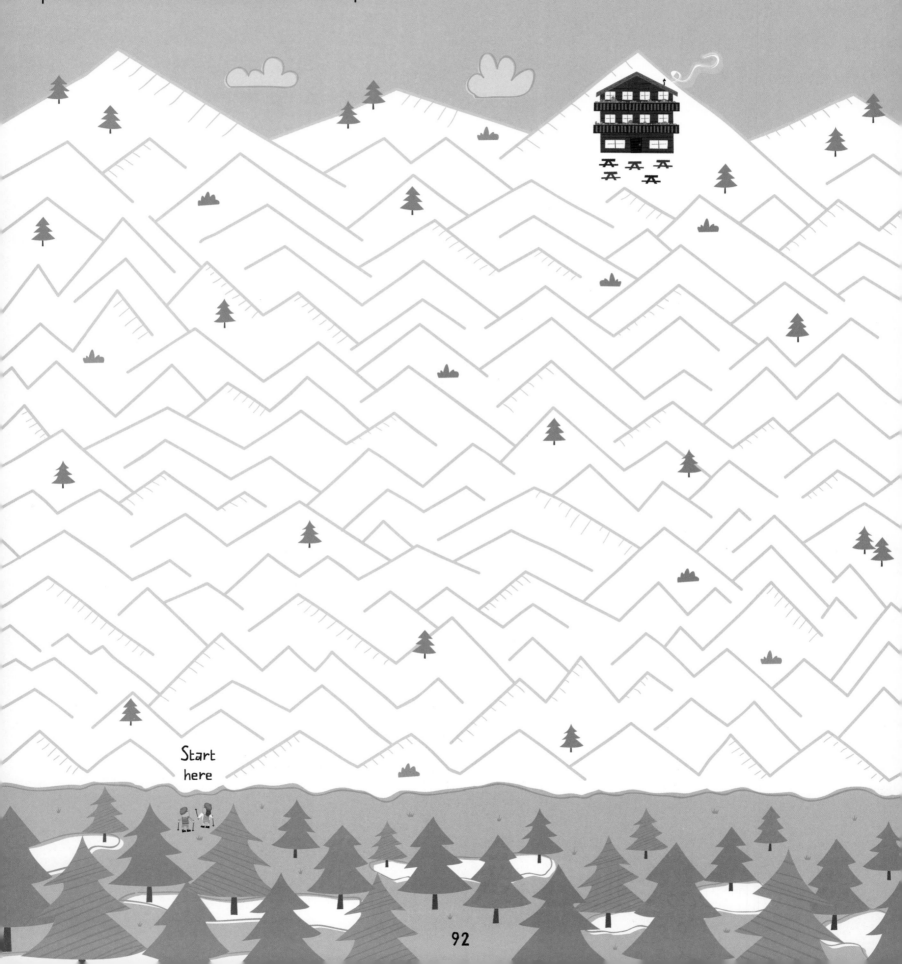

Start
here

Lady Mary's gardens

Enter Lady Mary's gardens through the iron gate and find your way to the central fountain to feed the hungry fish. Please remember to keep off the grass.

Fish Pond

Plumbing puzzle

Which pipe will carry water
uninterrupted to the bathtub?
(The water can flow in
any direction as long as
its path is not blocked.)

Apple orchard

Help the duck gather exactly six fallen apples on her way home. She can't take the same path twice or meet a hungry fox.

Mother and cub

Lead the mother polar bear back to her cub without crossing any of the cracks in the ice.

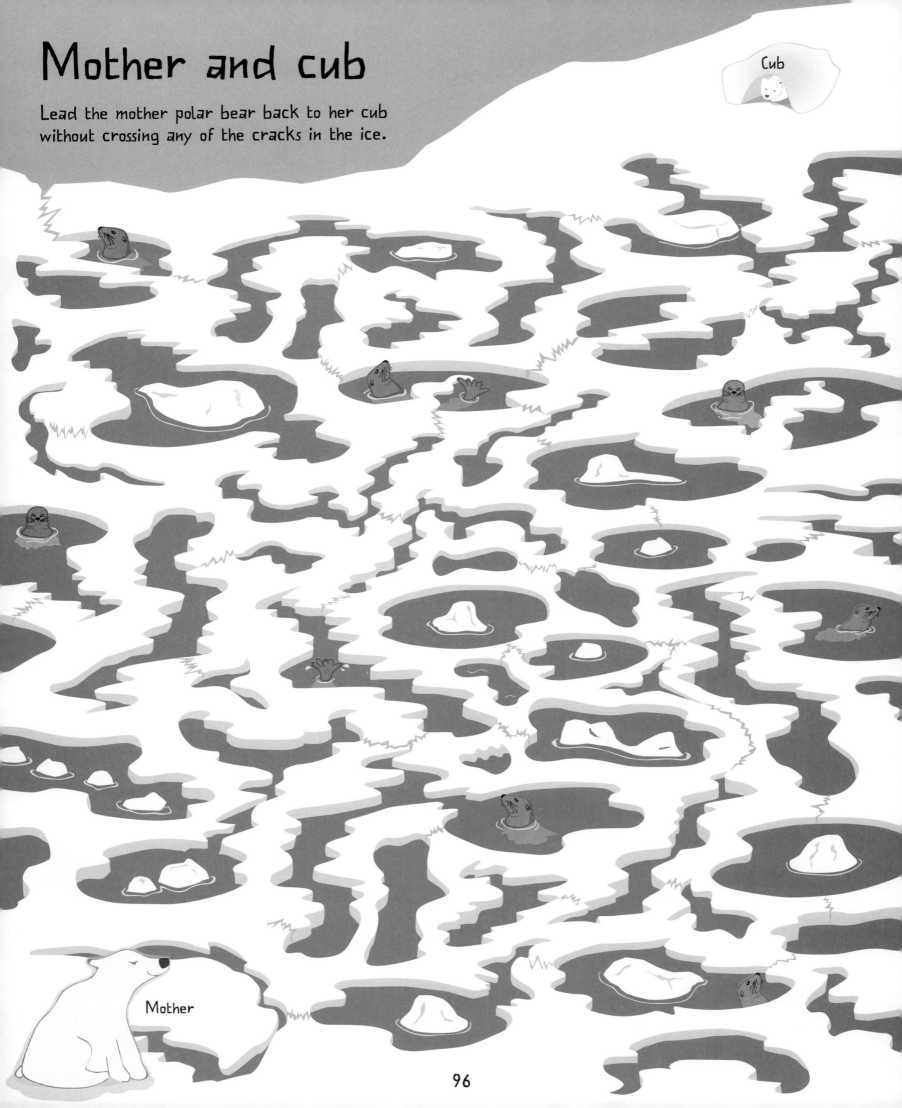

Cub

Mother

Suitcase search

Ben has lost his big, round, green suitcase.
Can you spot it, and help him to weave
his way through the stacks
of cases to find it?

Ben

Nuts and bolts

Starting at the wrench, see if you can find a way to move around the machine to tighten every nut. You can't travel along any path more than once.

Nuts look like this.

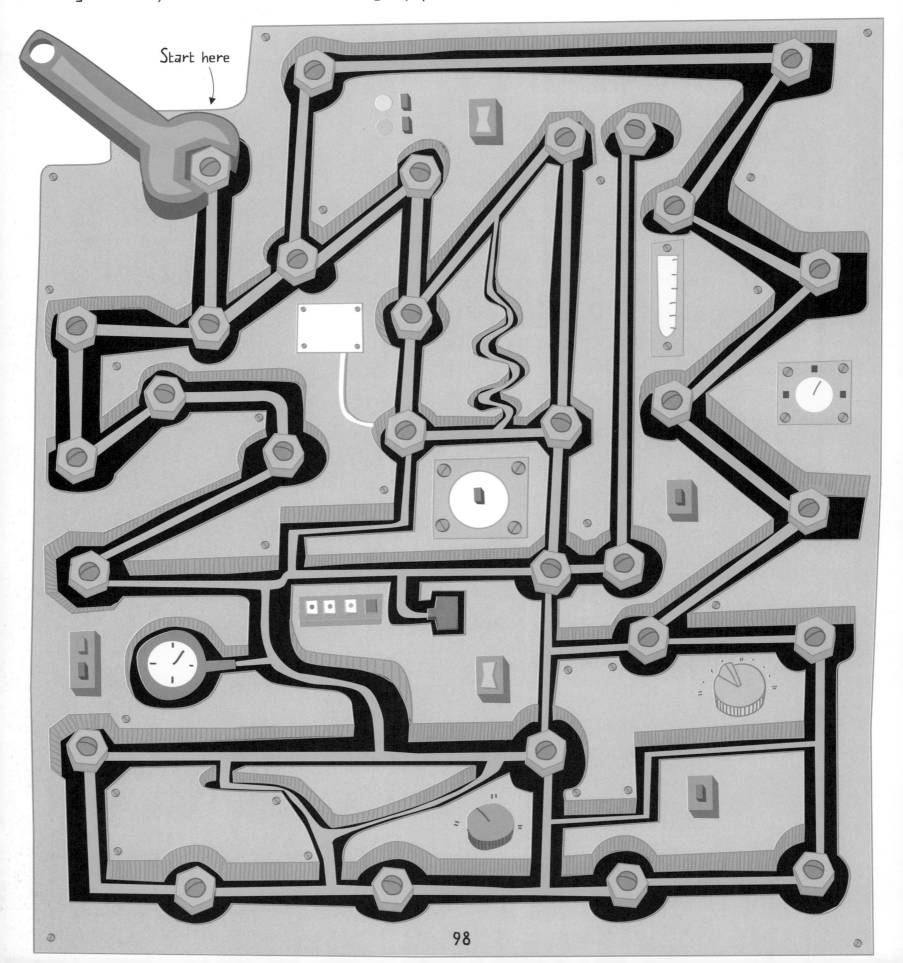

Start here

Circuit search

Help Robbie the robot find his way through the circuit maze to Rodney.
He can only change direction where there is a dot.

Rodney

Robbie

Resort route

The little red car is heading for the Seaside Beach Resort – but it's getting lost in all the tiny, twisty streets. Which way should it go?

Start here

SEASIDE
BEACH RESORT

Run, rabbit, run

Timmy the rabbit can only run along hedgerows —
and he's too nervous to pass any fields with animals
in them. He can run past gates, but only if they
are closed. See if you can lead him to the woods.

Timmy

Woods

Mysterious mansion

Help! How can Spike get out of this spooky house? Starting in the attic, he must use every staircase or ladder once only. He must creep through every room but he may only go once through any doorway. Can he escape before he loses his nerve?

Spike

Sticky spider's web

Quick! See if you can weave your way between the sticky threads to save the frantic flies before the spider reaches them.

Start here

Snap-happy Sarah

Sarah wants to photograph all 16 domed buildings for her school project. Lead her to the front of each one, without taking any path more than once.

Sarah

Penguin in peril

Pedro the penguin has left his surfboard back on the island. Guide him there safely between the waves, avoiding sharks, and other penguins.

Pedro

Market day

Carefully choose the route that lets you pick up all the shopping on the list in the right order. You shouldn't take any path twice, and remember to finish with an ice cream.

1 Pair of boots
2 Apples
3 Cheese
4 Flowers
5 Bread
6 Balloon
7 Umbrella
8 Eggs
9 Kite
10 Fish
11 Ice cream!

Start here

ices

BOOTS

Cheese   Fruit & Veg   Flowers   FISH

BLOOMS   BAKERY

BREAD   BALLOONS

Balloons

Umbrellas   Kites

Farm Eggs

BOOKS   GIFTS

Desert gold

Which underground passage will
lead you to the treasure chamber?

Start here

Start here

Runaway rollercoaster

Which route will lead the runaway rollercoaster safely to the end of the ride?

Start here

Tickets

End here

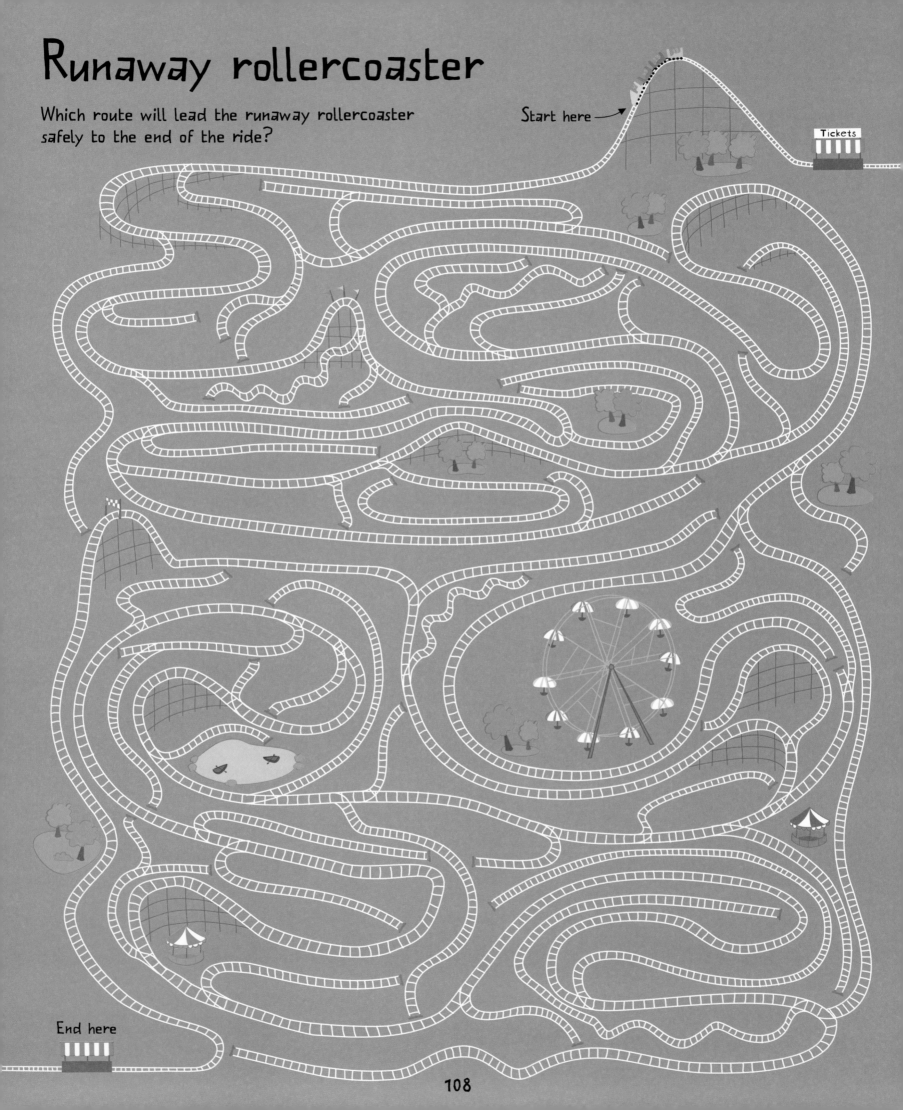

Coconuts ahoy!

The sailor needs to collect a coconut a day for a week-long voyage. Help him find a route across the ladders where every other tree he reaches has a coconut, so he can pick seven coconuts by the time he gets back to his boat. He can use each ladder only once.

End here

Start here

109

Puzzle pyramid

Starting at the bottom of the pyramid, can you find your way through the maze of passages to the pharaoh's tomb at the top? (Luckily, you have brought climbing equipment with you.)

Start here

Sheep search

Sheppie the sheepdog has lost his sheep. Which path should he take between the stone walls to find them?

Buzzing bees

Can you help these little bees through the honeycomb maze to visit their queen?
They can fit through any spaces in the white waxy walls.

Start here

Monster messengers

These monsters "talk" to each other by touching arms.
Which way will the message travel from the orange
monster at the edge to its friend in the middle?

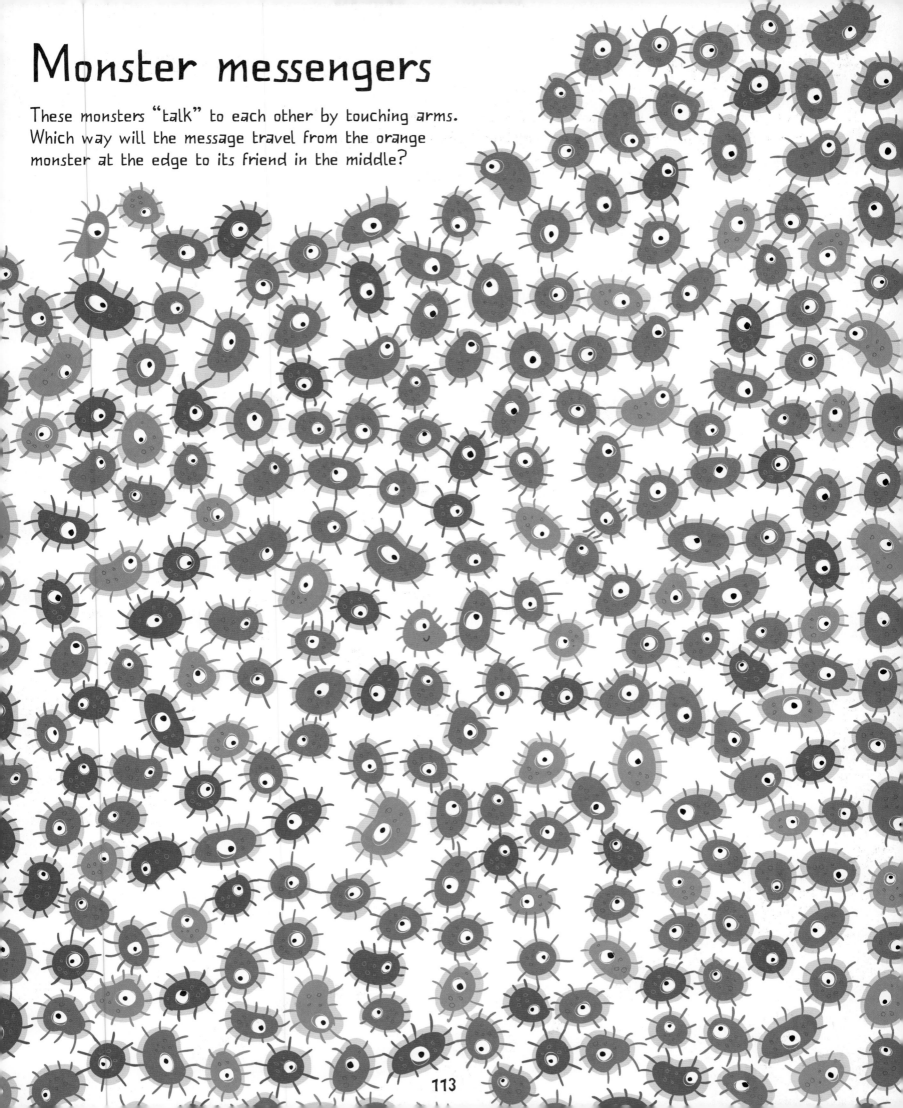

Art gallery

Your ticket for the art gallery lets you visit every room just once.
Plan a route that allows you to see every exhibit before you leave.

Volcano countdown

Quick! Escape the bubbling volcano before it erupts. The only safe place is the palm tree island. Watch out for sea serpents...

Parking puzzle

Find the nearest parking space for each car waiting at the entrance.
Drivers may only park between two cars of the same style as their own.
They can drive through empty parking spaces, but
only between cars of exactly the same shade as
theirs. And don't forget it's a one-way system!

ENTRANCE

Puzzling pattern

Find your way between the lines and shapes,
moving only through the white spaces.

Start

Finish

Testing tubes

This experiment is getting a little out of control.
Assist the scientist by finding the correct route
from the flask of green liquid, along the glass
tubing, to the bubbling water tank.

Start

Finish

Gold rush

The gold cart has rolled all the way down from the top of the mountain. Can you help the miner find a safe route down to fetch it? He can't step on or over cracks and must avoid broken ladders and bridges.

He will have to walk around cracks.

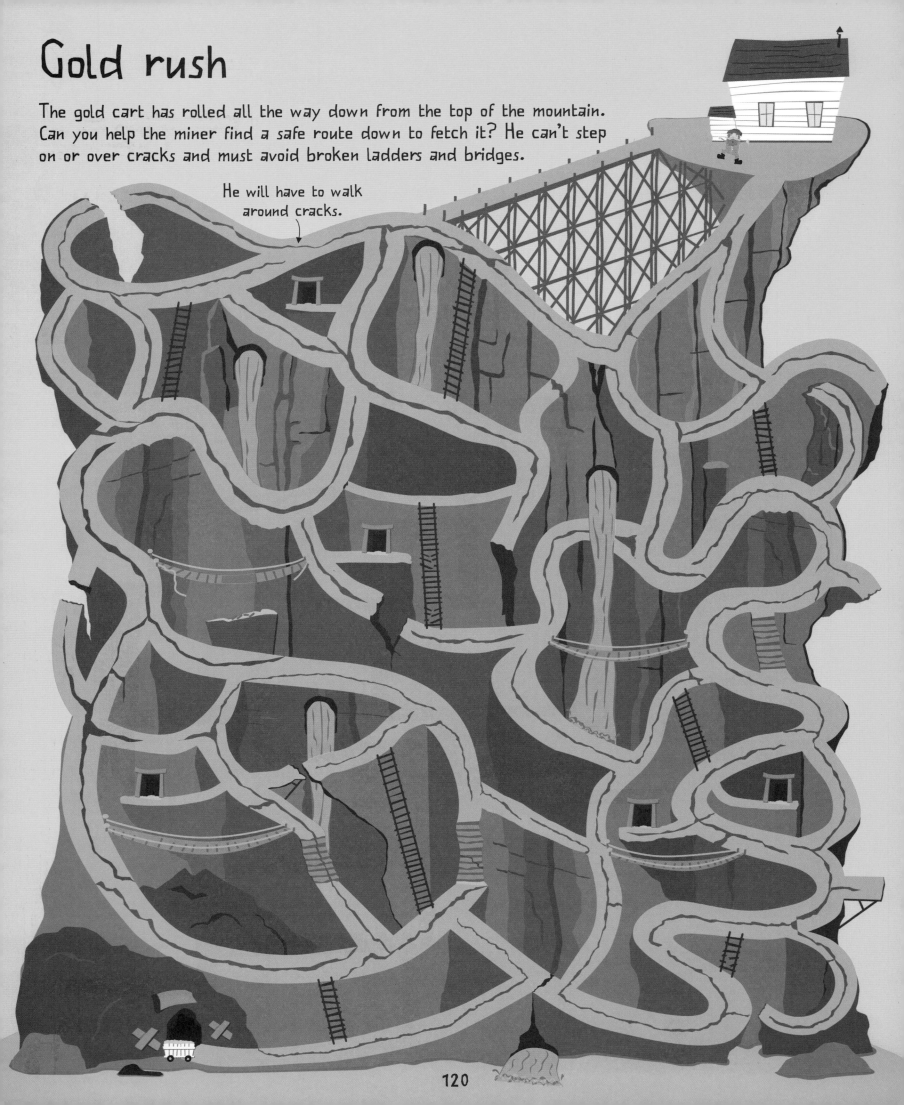

2. Turtle tangle   3. All the animals   4. Penguin playtime   5. Digger dilemma

6. Follow the herd   7. Marina maze   8. Anthill antics   9. Cloudy peril

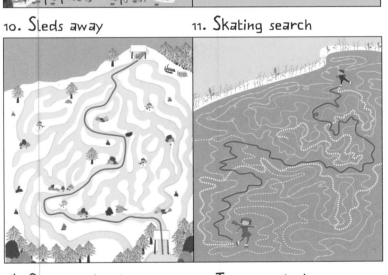

10. Sleds away   11. Skating search   12–13. On safari

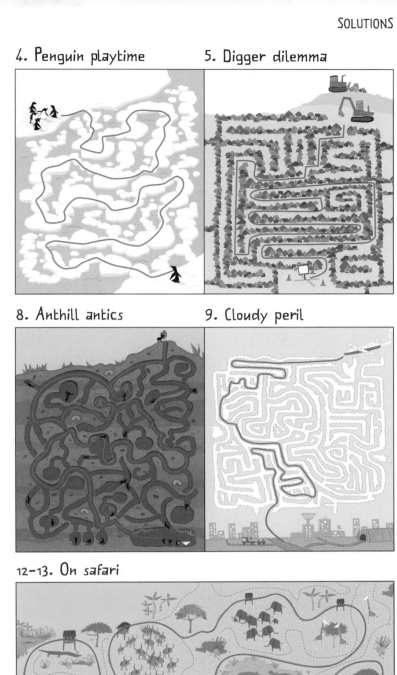

14. Graveyard getaway   15. Too many tools   16. The shelf run   17. Hidden surprise

22 doorways

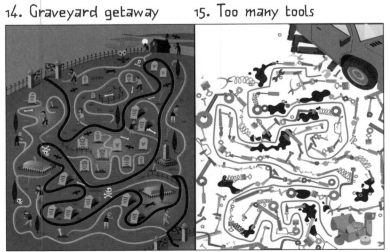

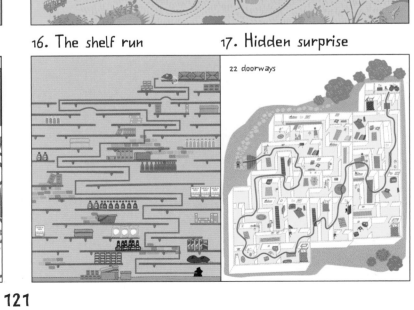

18-19. Busy beach

20. Traffic trouble

21. Spiny starfish

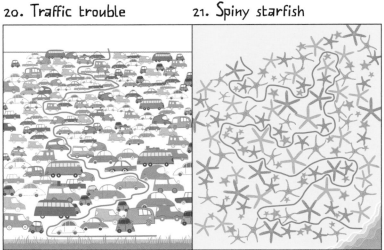

22. Fred's shed

23. Pecking hen

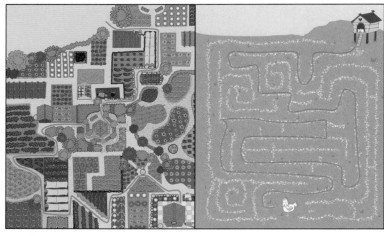

24-25. Farm visit

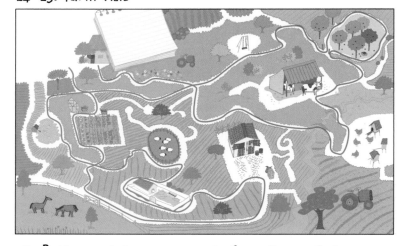

26. Rooftop ramble

27. Around the underground

28. Button match maze

29. Campsite confusion

30-31. Beware of the bears

32. Biking buddies

33. Midnight express

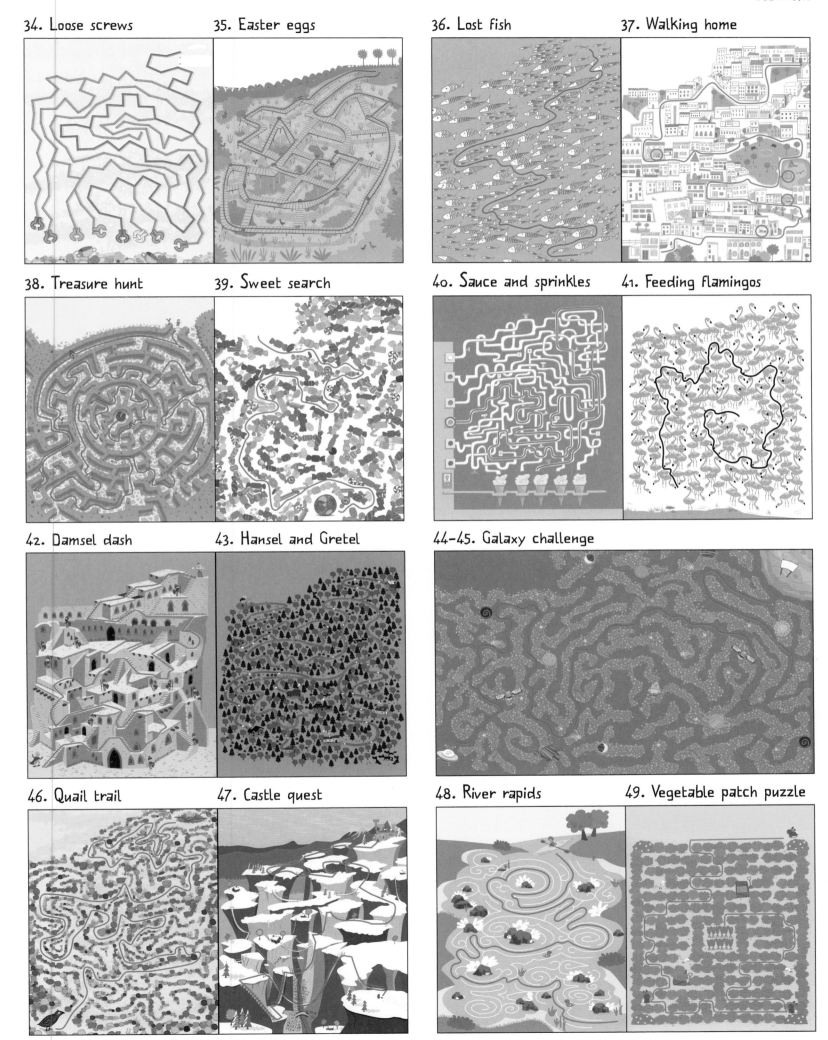

34. Loose screws
35. Easter eggs
36. Lost fish
37. Walking home
38. Treasure hunt
39. Sweet search
40. Sauce and sprinkles
41. Feeding flamingos
42. Damsel dash
43. Hansel and Gretel
44-45. Galaxy challenge
46. Quail trail
47. Castle quest
48. River rapids
49. Vegetable patch puzzle

50–51. Around the airport

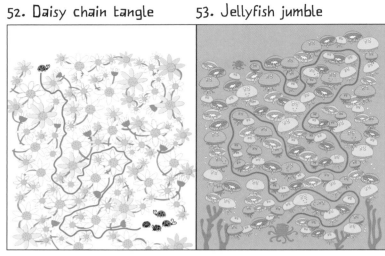

52. Daisy chain tangle

53. Jellyfish jumble

54. Snakes and ladders

55. Go, Billy goat!

56–57. Treasure Island

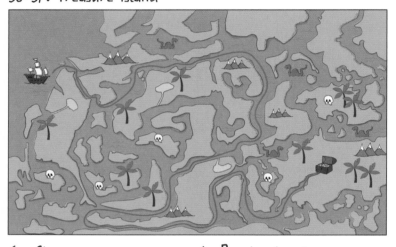

58. At the racetrack

59. Star search

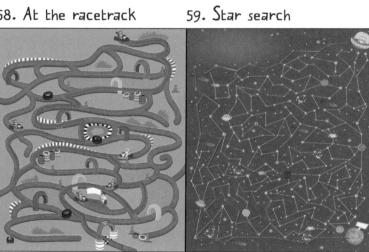

60. Chess mess

61. Puzzle planet

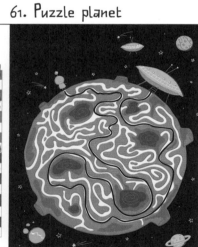

62. Milkshake-maker

63. Toy inspectors

Skateboard = 3
Ball = -1
Robot = 6

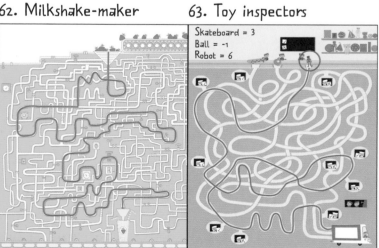

64–65. Santa's sleighride

66. Birds and branches

67. Pencil box muddle

68-69. Feed the cows

70. Flight plan

71. The Labyrinth

72-73. Lily pad race

Freddie will win

74. Desert disaster

75. Busy bus

76-77. Bear mountain

78. Zip, Zap, swap!

79. Fairground fun

80. Monkey puzzle

81. Hedgehog hurry

82. Camel confusion

83. Eye in the sky

84-85. A walk in the park

86. Route race

The orange car will win

87. Super slalom

88. Apple maze

Caspar will win

89. Construction chaos

90. Hungry hamster

91. Treetop tea party

92. Peaks and valleys

93. Lady Mary's gardens

94. Plumbing puzzle

95. Apple orchard

96. Mother and cub

97. Suitcase search

98. Nuts and bolts

99. Circuit search

100. Resort route

101. Run, rabbit, run

102. Mysterious mansion

103. Sticky spider's web

104. Snap-happy Sarah

105. Penguin in peril

106. Market day

107. Desert gold

108. Runaway rollercoaster

109. Coconuts ahoy!

110. Puzzle pyramid

111. Sheep search

112. Buzzing bees

113. Monster messengers

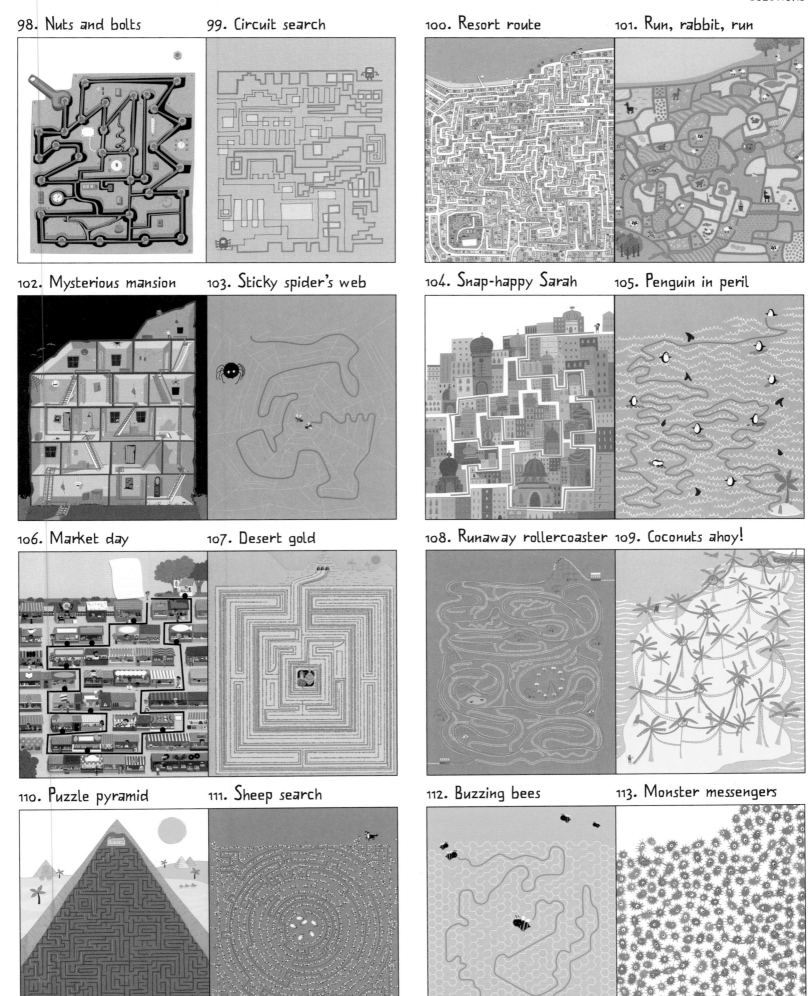

114. Art gallery

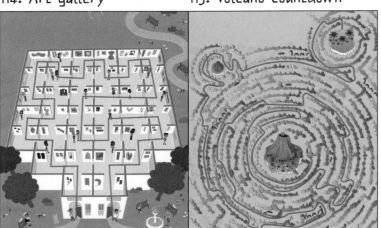

115. Volcano countdown

116–117. Parking puzzle

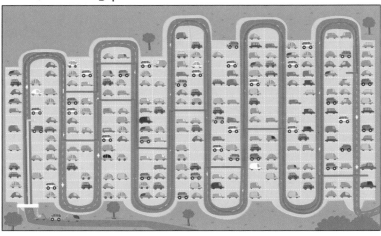

118. Puzzling pattern

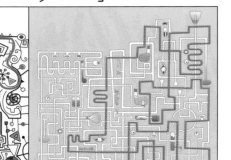

119. Testing tubes

120. Gold rush

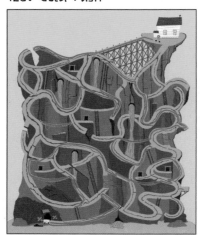

Acknowledgements

Additional designs by Laura Hammonds,
Marc Maynard, Tim Ki-Kydd and Keith Furnival

Cover design by Candice Whatmore

Edited by Sam Taplin and Kirsteen Robson

With thanks to our maze testers:
Zachary Boachie-Barrance, Janey Harold, Faye Jones and Jack Middleton